BREEDING

SNAKES

IN CAPTIVITY

Pet Reference Series No. 3

ROBERT J. RICHES

ARCO PUBLISHING CO, INC.
New York

Published by ARCO Publishing Company, Inc.
219 Park Avenue South, New York, N.Y. 10003

Library of Congress Cataloging in Publication Data

Riches, Robert J.
    Breeding snakes in captivity.

    (Pet reference series; no. 3)
    Bibliography: p.
    Includes index.
    1. Snakes--Breeding. I. Title.
SF459.S5R5   639'.39'2   76-6930
ISBN 0-915096-01-3

Arco order number: 04056-4 (paper)
                    04057-2 (LR cloth)

This book has been set in Palatino 10 point by Photocomp, Inc., using a computerized process and printed in America by the Great Outdoors Press, St. Petersburg, Florida.

ACKNOWLEDGEMENT

The Author wishes to express thanks to just two people; his wife, Gladys, for her infinite patience with a husband who is always "with his animals", and to Ross Allen for his encouragement without which not a word would have been written.

THE AUTHOR

Bob Riches, now in his early forties, has been a reptile enthusiast since his schooldays, and since that time has maintained an assorted collection of specimens. He gained experience by keeping many varieties of snakes, lizards, turtles and crocodilians. In the early 1960's he decided to turn his attention to attempting to breed the American Garter and Water snakes under controlled indoor conditions. This book is the result of several years of leisure-time preoccupation with this project.

Contents

1. INTRODUCTION

There has, in recent times, been an upsurge of interest in the breeding of the rarer animals in zoological collections and exhibitions. Zoos are now prepared to finance research into the conditions necessary to breed these creatures in close captivity. It is no longer acceptable for a zoo merely to exhibit specimens and replace them when they die, with animals from the wild. Not only from the point of view of expense and the increasing difficulty of obtaining replacement specimens from foreign countries (and, indeed, some indigenous animals), but also to some extent to justify the very existence of zoos. It is hyprocrisy for a zoo to support and foster the idea of conservation if it is, by the way it is managed, one of the causes for the depletion of animal stocks in the wild state. The destruction of wild habitats is another reason for the development of breeding programs. Reptiles are an exceptional problem from a conservation angle, as it is difficult in virtually any country to stop their wholesale slaughter. Even if they have no commercial value, as in the case of small harmless snakes, they are killed merely because they are snakes. Television wildlife programs are making a useful contribution in attempting to educate the general public to a more reasonable and realistic attitude toward reptiles, but overall it seems at times a losing battle. It is easy to gain public sympathy to wildlife conservation when the subjects concerned are appealing furry animals, but a different matter altogether to excite the same feeling for a threatened species of snake, however innocuous. With the continuing human population increase and the consequent destruction and pollution of the natural environment, even reptiles that were once commonplace are rapidly becoming a rare sight.

I chose to confine my studies almost exclusively to the American Garter and Water snakes for several reasons. One reason being that they are livebearers (the European Natrix are all egg-layers), and another that these snakes are easier to feed. Unlike their European relatives, they are quite prepared to accept dead food or even just pieces of raw fish. It can be an almost impossible task at times to keep available a constant supply of living amphibians or small fish, if there are more than just one or two snakes to consider. A further important reason was that I considered them to be attractive snakes, subject to much colour variation, and well worth a place in a reptile collection. I realize that in the United States the Garter and Water snakes generally are not in any danger of extinction, with the exception perhaps of the very beautiful San Francisco Garter snake *(Thamnophis sirtalis tetrataenia)*, which is at present on the United States list of Endangered Fish and Wildlife. Steps should be taken now, by intensive breeding projects, to ensure that this sub-species, probably second only to the Corn or Red Rat snake *(Elaphe guttata guttata)* for beauty, does not die out.

The breeding behavior of reptiles is for the vast majority of species an unopened book. The conditions necessary for breeding are only now being studied in any detail, and certain American zoos seem to be making good progress in this respect. Research into the subject should not, I feel, be confined to the rarer and more exotic species, as the commonplace indigenous reptiles of today could well become the rarities of tomorrow. Great emphasis seems to have been placed on various forms of infra-red and ultra-violet heating and lighting as indispensable aids to promote breeding, and although I concede that these are necessary where certain types of lizards are concerned, I am certain that for many snakes they are not.

In my experiments with crossing sub-species of American Water snakes I produced intergrades which would not occur naturally in the wild state, as the ranges of the original snakes would not overlap. Any "unnatural" crosses like this should be confined to reptile collections and not released in the wild for any

2

reason, to cause possible confusion to taxonomists studying range limits.

I have found no difficulty in disposing of surplus specimens, as collectors and zoological institutions are only too keen to acquire sound, healthy stock free of parasites and blemishes. 'Captive hatched' babies are better suited to captive conditions than their parents. This brings me to the commercial possibilities of the snake breeding. Apart from private collectors and zoos there are many colleges, universities and schools where snakes are required for educational purposes as living specimens, or subjects for dissection. It is a far better state of affairs, to my mind, that their supplies should come from snakes bred in captivity rather than specimens taken from the wild. If one is able to breed something out of the ordinary, say for example the all-black (melanistic) Garter snake, then there is a ready market. I must stress, however, that the commercial aspect in my particular case was merely a relatively unimportant sideline to dispose of snakes surplus to requirements, although I have to admit the money obtained was useful to subsidize the heating and lighting bills, and the acquisition of additional sub-species. It is feasible that done on a large enough scale "snake farming" could be a commercial proposition.

What I have been able to find out about the controlled breeding of snakes is obviously just a beginning. There is much more study necessary; I hope others will be encouraged to take up similar projects and no doubt improve upon my methods.

Bristol, England. July 1973.   Robert J. Riches.

2. ABOUT SNAKES

Snakes, together with lizards, crocodiles, turtles and the lizard-like tuatara from New Zealand form the class of animals known as reptiles, and in the scale of evolution they appear between the amphibians and the birds. Reptiles, were, at one stage in pre-history, the dominant terrestrial vertebrate life, and most people are familiar with the popular reconstructions of the gigantic dinosaurs which roamed the earth during that period referred to as the "Age of Reptiles". This period came to an end about seventy million years ago, yet some reptiles have survived virtually unchanged to the present day. The crocodile, for example, was a contemporary of the dinosaurs, and after millions of years of existence is only now threatened with extinction — by man; not only by direct killing but by man's use (or more often abuse) of the remaining natural areas of the world. So it is with the larger turtles killed for eating, or the lizards and snakes sought after to manufacture leather shoes and handbags from their brightly patterned skins. Modern reptiles comprise about 6000 species, but at the present rate of destruction a large number will pass to extinction before the turn of the century. The particular features which distinguish reptiles from other classes of animals are as follows:-

1. Poikilothermy or "coldbloodedness". This is the lack of an internal mechanism for regulating the body temperature, and means that the temperature of a snake, or other reptile, is governed to a very large extent by the prevailing temperature of its environment. In a warm place the reptile is warm, while in a cold

place the creature may be so chilled that it is torpid and unable to move or function properly. Most reptiles are found in the warmer regions of the world, and those living in cooler temperate regions are forced to hibernate below ground during cold winter months. Recent research has shown that in the wild, reptiles are able to control their body temperature to quite a surprising extent, and keep it constant within a few degrees for extended periods. This is done by basking in the sun until the preferred temperature is achieved, and then moving into shade before overheating occurs. When the body temperature drops the animal again takes advantage of the sun's rays or lies on sun-warmed earth. By constant movement of this sort a reptile can remain at its favorite temperature for a certain length of time, but of course this procedure can only be put into effect when sunshine (and adequate shade cover) is available. It is an interesting fact that in some reptiles the preferred temperature is very close to that which proves fatal to them by overheating.

2. Reptiles breathe atmospheric air by means of lungs; they do not possess gills like fish or amphibian larvae.

3. They are covered by a scaly skin or scutes.

4. The eggs are laid on land and are well supplied with large quantities of yolk, resembling birds in this respect. Some reptiles are live-bearing in that the eggs (in a thin-walled sac instead of a thick leathery shell) are retained in the mother's body, and young either break out of the sacs immediately before birth, or emerge soon after the complete sacs have been deposited.

5. Upon hatching or at birth young reptiles are essentially similar in shape and habits to their parents. They do not undergo a metamorphosis from a larva stage as in the case of tadpoles into frogs.

These are the main features which characterise the reptiles, although there are many other features of skeletal and internal organ structure of interest to the serious student of herpetology.

Snakes and lizards are very closely related reptiles, and although placed in separate suborders (Ophidia and Lacertilia) they are both members of the order Squamata. Snakes are among the most specialized of reptiles having evolved from lizards and adapted, with a high degree of success, to a life without limbs. Their degree of success can be appreciated when one realises that they include the most expert burrowers, swimmers and climbers in the animal world. Their internal organs have had to undergo modification in order to conform to the elongated body shape. For example snakes have only one functional lung, the right, and the left one is either altogether absent or reduced to a tiny rudiment. However, the functional right lung extends for more than half the length of the snake's body.

Snakes excite much interest over their methods of feeding and obtaining prey. To an uninitiated person the first experience of observing a small Water snake swallowing a large frog, or a slender King snake engulfing an adult mouse is an awe-inspiring and unbelieveable sight. It seems an impossible operation, and on a par with forcing a loaf of bread into a bicycle innertube. This technique is possible because the jaw bones are joined to the skull and each other by elastic ligaments which allow them to dislocate, and with the help of backward-pointing teeth the jaws move independently to pull the snakes's mouth out around the prey. Once it is past the mouth the strong muscles of the oesophagus take over.

Many types of snakes have no special method of killing prey, merely swallowing it alive so that it succumbs by suffocation or the action of digestive juices. Other types of snakes have developed the skill of constricting their prey, using their muscular coils to kill them quickly and efficiently before any counter attack can be made. With such intended meals as rats or mice a snake can be badly bitten if its actions are slow or clumsy, but normally the victim dies within seconds from a combination of suffocation and shock.

The third method of overpowering prey is by the use of venom. At its most efficient (for example, the rattlesnake) it enables the reptile to strike at its intended meal, inject venom, and then quickly withdraw to wait for the victim to succumb, without the risk of retaliation and possible injury to the snake. The venomous snakes have been a source of wonderment and fear to man since early times, and even today they take their toll of human lives particularly in India and southeast Asia.

The venom itself is a complex liquid composed of enzymes and protein-like substances which have devastating effects on various types of animal tissue. They are either mainly haematoxic (that is, causing disintegration of tissues including blood corpuscles and the bloodvessel linings), or neurotoxic (acting on the nervous system, especially that relating to the heart and respiratory system). There are ingredients which cause profuse bleeding in the tissues, or alternatively others which act as coagulents to produce thromboses. Each species of venomous snake has its own distinct combination of venom ingredients; that of vipers and rattlesnakes is predominatly haematoxic, whilst that of cobras, mambas and kraits is neurotoxic in nature.

The venom glands are situated in the snake's upper jaw below and behind the eyes. Venom is injected by means of grooved or hollow fangs, which in the Viperidae are virtually hypodermic needles.

The back-fanged snakes are not generally considered dangerous to man, as the position of the short grooved fangs in the back of the upper jaw means that a chewing action is necessary to bring them into play. The venom then travels along the fang grooves, and although adequate to paralyse small prey is not very potent as far as humans are concerned, with the possible exception of that of the African Boomslang.

The Elapids (for example cobras and kraits) have fangs in the front of the jaws although these are fairly short and fixed. To inject sufficient venom a definite bite and sometimes a chewing action is necessary to achieve maximum penetration. However, the fangs are hollow and venom is injected under pressure, and to man a bite is a very serious matter.

The snakes of the family Viperidae, which includes vipers and rattlesnakes, have very long fangs which form a first-class hypodermic injection system capable of forcing venom deep into the tissues of prey with a lightning stabbing movement. The fangs of, for instance, a large Gaboon Viper can be as long as two inches. The fangs fold back along the inside of the upper jaw when not in use, but when the snake is about to strike they are

Position of Fangs and Venom Glands.

Viperidae
Rattlesnakes and Vipers. Fangs fold back when not in use.

Elapidae
Cobras, Kraits and Mambas. Fixed fangs.

Colubridae
Boomslang, certain tree snakes, etc.; Most Colubrids are harmless.

A. Ringhal
   (spitting fang)

B. Non-spitting fang.

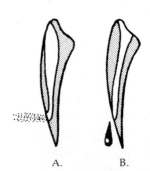

A.   B.

erected by muscular action.

The venom apparatus is used not only for obtaining food, but also as a defence mechanism against would-be predators. To this end the so-called "spitting cobras" or Ringhals have the fangs adapted to be able to spray out a fine mist of venom to a distance of about eight feet, causing temporary blindness and a great deal of pain to an attacker should the venom reach its eyes.

It is recommended that venomous snakes are only kept in captivity by experienced herpetologists in research laboratories or zoological stations. In the private home they are a potential danger to family, friends and neighbors. However careful one is with a snake collection escapes are always a possibility.

The author's view is that there is so much research to be done on the many species of harmless snakes, that there is no necessity for the amateur to become too concerned with venomous varieties, in fact, it is highly desirable that he does not do so!

For amateur herpetologists who wish to pursue the scientific approach to this subject, the following outline to snake classification has been included. It must be appreciated that scientific work in current progress, and the varying opinions of scientific works results in continual changes being made to relative positions of some species. These are often of a minor character as far as the amateur is concerned, but may well be important in an exact sense.

Phylum	Chordata	
Subphylum	Vertebrata	
Class	Reptilia	
Order	Squamata	
Suborder	Ophidia	
Family	Typhlopidae	Blind snakes or worm-snakes. Small harmless burrowing species.
	Leptotyphlopidae	Blind snakes, worm-snakes or thread-snakes superficially like Typhlopidae.

Aniliidae	Includes Subfamilies Aniliinae (pipe snakes), Uropeltinae (shield-tailed snakes — harmless burrowers with enlarged spiny shield on the tail tip), and Xenopeltinae (sunbeam snake).
Boidae	Subfamilies Pythoninae (pythons), Boinae (boas, anaconda), Erycinae (sand boas) and Bolyerinae (boas from Mauritius).
Achrochordidae	Elephant's trunk (or Wart) snake. Water snakes with specialized granular scales.
Colubridae	The majority of snakes are contained in this family, which embraces a number of subfamilies. Most are harmless, but others are back-fanged and mildly venomous.
Elapidae	Family of highly venomous snakes with fangs fixed and relatively small. Includes cobras, kraits, mambas, etc.
Hydrophiidae	Sea snakes. Closely allied to cobras.
Viperidae	Highly venomous snakes with well developed moveable fangs. Includes Old World vipers, rattlesnakes and pit-vipers.

3. ACCOMMODATION

The very first consideration when contemplating keeping any type of livestock is satisfactory accomodation, and when it is planned to breed snakes then it has to be accepted that large numbers of reasonably small cages will be needed. As space is usually at a premium, a system has to be devised to get the largest number of cages into the smallest possible space, yet making sure that each and every cage is readily accessible to attend to the needs of the inmates and for cleaning purposes. Cages can be stacked directly one on top of another, and if they are front-opening this presents no problem. If, however, aquarium tanks are used then access to the lower tanks means removing all those above, and this can be a very irritating and time-wasting business. It had been found most convenient for access, and indeed heating and lighting economy measures to arrange the cages in pairs (see Fig.). With this arrangement the position of the cages in each pair can be reversed every twelve hours, and the inmates of each cage will have twelve hours of bright lighting and a similar period of subdued lighting or semi-darkness, with the overall temperature having little variation. The pairs of tanks can be arranged on shelves; a very convenient type being the banks of adjustable metal shelving designed for use in offices or storerooms.

The best size of cage for adult stock is 24" x 12" x 12", one cage being adequate for several female or say six male specimens (in both Garter and Water snakes the females are considerably longer and bulkier than the males). For the baby snakes a number

11

of 12" x 8" x 8" tanks are recommended. As these babies are quite small at birth it is reasonable to keep as many as twelve in a small cage. As they grow so the number of snakes per cage is reduced.

Fiberglass cage. This type of cage has no rough spots for the snake to rub its nose against and it is easy to clean.

The choice of materials for the construction of cages is wide. The author has favored metal framed aquarium tanks as these are easy to wash out and sterilize if the need arises, but there are on the market suitable cages of plastic and fiberglass materials which would have the advantage of weighing very little compared with aquaria of similar size. This could be quite an important consideration if one is thinking of having a number of tanks on shelving, as the combined weight of several metal framed glass tanks can be quite alarming.

(If costs are a consideration, local pet stores often have used aquariums for sale, usually 'leakers'. These are more than adequate for housing snakes, and cost considerably less than new aquariums.)

Adequate ventilation to each cage is necessary. If small aquarium tanks are utilized a perforated hardboard (pegboard)

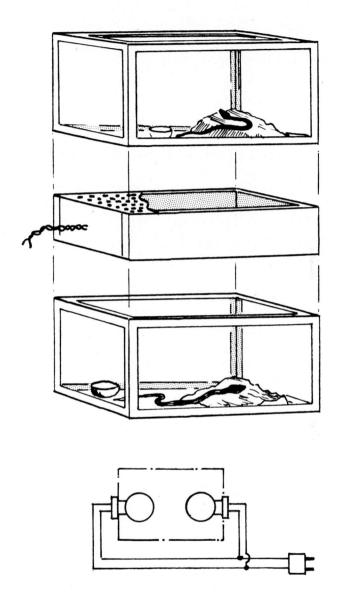

ABOVE:— Two-tier system for small cages. Middle section (wood with pegboard top) incorporates two low-wattage light bulbs for heating and lighting.

BELOW:— Arrangement of bulbs in wooden section. Wiring is such that the failure of one bulb will not affect the other.

lid is ideal. Perforated zinc or metal screening has the big draw-back in that snakes will rub their snouts raw on it. Any sharp edges of cage framing, electrical fitting or even screwheads inside the cage must be filed smooth to avoid self injury by the snakes.

TEMPERATURES.

The approach to the question of temperatures at which to keep one's stock depends largely on where it is intended to locate the "snake room", and also the local climate. At the author's home in Bristol, England, the climate was such that heating of some sort was necessary for most of the year and could only be dispensed with during warm spells in midsummer. Generally, one should aim to have a daytime temperature of 75 to 85 degrees Fahrenheit, with facilities to lower this at night to not lower than 60 degrees, if this is considered necessary. It was found that the most satisfactory method of dealing with temperature arrange-ments in the north-facing room used to house the author's collec-tion was to keep the whole room at a constant 60 degrees, by means of a thermostatically controlled electric radiator. All cages were additionally heated by small wattage (15w. or 25w.) electric light bulbs to raise the temperature by approximately 20 degrees over the room level. Temperature variation could then be given to specimens requiring it by the simple expedient of switching off the light bulbs and allowing the cage temperature to drop to room temperature. In the event of light bulbs failing and the fact not being discovered for a while there was no danger of the snakes concerned becoming chilled, as the lowest limit to which the temperature could drop was 60 degrees Fahrenheit.

If it is not possible to provide continuous background heat-ing then, of course, larger wattage bulbs will be necessary in the cages. A temperature drop, when required, will necessitate changing to lower wattage bulbs. Here a word of warning is in order — do not use high wattage bulbs where snakes are able to lie on, coil around or rest against them. Snakes can sustain fatal burn injuries in this way, and even if the burns are not serious the resultant disfiguring scars ruin the snake's appearance. It is bet-ter to use two medium wattage bulbs than one of high wattage.

Specimens can be kept at a constant 75 to 85 degrees F, night and day, without suffering any ill effects. Temperatures however must be varied when one is considering a female snake about to produce her offspring. If she has no choice but to give birth to her young in a hot, dry atmosphere (when probably one is not on hand to give immediate attention) then heavy losses can be expected. This topic is discussed in a later chapter.

FURNISHINGS

It is assumed that the snakes in any breeding program will not be on public view, and therefore cage furnishings can be strictly utilitarian. When large numbers of small cages are being maintained, the principal consideration is ease of cleaning, and to this end the author has used sheets of newspaper as flooring. This is absorbent and can be changed quickly when it is soiled. The only other items necessary are a piece of curved cork bark, or something similar, under which the snakes can hide, and a small water dish. It is particularly stressed that a small dish (for drinking purposes only) is adequate, as apart from the time immediately before a snake is due to produce young or to slough its epidermis the cage must be kept dry. A large water dish will encourage snakes to soak in the water for extended periods, and also will increase the general humidity level in the cage. It is appreciated that in nature the garter and water snakes are found in marshes and beside streams and lakes, but they have ample opportunity to dry out completely by basking in the sun. In a continually damp cage these snakes become very susceptible to severe skin complaints which quite often prove fatal.

PARASITES

Snake collections can very easily become infested with mites. This is a serious matter not only for the obvious irritation to the snakes, but for the fact that these pests can transmit diseases to stock.

Every effort should be made to ensure that an infestation does not occur. All new stock (particularly that purchased from dealers) should be quarantined and completely isolated from the main collection until it is absolutely sure that they are free of external parasites. Mites can spread throughout a collection during the course of a single day, causing considerable extra work in the disinfecting of a whole snake room. With stocks of very small snakes the question of infestation is even more serious, as they can literally be tormented to death by mites.

Until recently the methods used for clearing mites have been drastic and time-consuming; sterilizing tanks with disinfectant, boiling water dishes and cork bark, and treating specimens with paraffin rubs (use too little and it was non-effective; too much and there was the problem of the snakes' scales lifting off). Another way was to immerse a specimen in water for extended periods to drown the mites. In short, to be completely effective the treatment needed to be so severe that the snakes themselves were in danger. The insect sprays containing DDT proved to be as efficient as killing reptiles as they were with insects, mites and ticks.

Experiments have been carried out recently by a number of herpetologists using the Shell "no-Pest" strip (called "Vapona" in Britain). Providing this product is used in a sensible fashion it can clear mite infestations almost overnight. The author has used it to clear mites (and ticks) from Garter, Water, Rat and King snakes with no ill effects to the specimens themselves. The method is to cut a small piece of the strip (approximately a half-inch square), put this into a small plastic or metal container in which a number of holes have been punched, and suspend it from the top of the affected cage for twelve hours only. The specimens must not be able to touch the piece of strip in any way. This treatment can be repeated a few days later to make sure all pests are killed. The half-inch square is adequate for a 24" x 12" x 12" cage.

Used with discretion the strip can be very useful; used carelessly there is a real chance of killing snakes and parasites at the same time.

4. FOODS & FEEDING

It is obvious that the best type of food for the snakes is that which they would normally take under wild conditions, such as small freshwater fish, frogs, toads and earthworms. If it is possible to maintain a steady supply of these items then there is no problem with feeding your snakes, but if such supplies are difficult or likely to be spasmodic, then other arrangements are necessary. In the author's case it was only possible to obtain a couple of dozen minnows at a time, and this only on occasional weekends when time could be found to drive out to a nearby river and set out minnow traps. So an alternative diet for the stock was essential. Early experience with Eastern Garter snakes had shown that although the babies eagerly accepted earthworms this food in itself was not enough, as the snakes very quickly displayed signs of rickets and eventually died. Young snakes must have an adequate calcium content in their food if they are to develop normally. Eventually, a diet was devised which resulted in hundreds of young snakes being reared successfully. In summer and fall minnows were given whenever possible, but the main diet consisted of strips of raw plaice or flounder. The whole fish would be cut into narrow strips at right angles to the backbone, resulting in a series of pieces of varying length each containing a quantity of bone. The pieces from near the tail end were suitable for very small snakes, and the larger strips could be fed to the adults. The bones in the fish provided the necessary calcium.

The important food supplement was a water-soluble multivitamin preparation known as "Abidec". A few drops of this concentrate was dissolved into the drinking water of every cage containing baby snakes. The adult specimens had a drop of "Abidec" on a piece of fish at each of their once-weekly meals. In winter and spring when minnows were very difficult to obtain it was possible to get herring from the fish merchant, and these were used (sliced up into sections containing bone) as an exclusive diet. The use of herring, when in season, was mainly an economy measure as they were very cheap in comparison with plaice or flounder, but the added advantage with them was that large garter snakes and medium to large water snakes could quite easily swallow whole fish. In America, smelt or whiting can be obtained easily. The vitamin supplement is necessary because fish fillets contain no vitamin A. The "Abidec" vitamin supplement was given the whole year round.

The proof that the diet as outlined was satisfactory is in the numbers of baby snakes reared successfully, and the fact that these babies grew fast. In some cases they matured at a surprisingly early age. Appendix 2 details one of the early attempts which although resulting in only one baby being reared indicated how quickly snakes could be brought to sexual maturity. The earliest maturity recorded by the author relates to a male Two-striped garter snake (*Thamnophis couchi hammondi*), which reached a length of 18⅝ inches and was endeavouring to mate with a young female companion at the age of only five months.

Garter snakes can be given earthworms whenever available as long as these do not form a major part of their food intake. The eastern garters (*Thamnophis sirtalis subspecies*) eagerly take these, but they are usually refused by the western varieties (*Thamnophis elegans, couchi, etc.*) and almost all water snakes. Some garters will take pieces of raw meat, although a number find it somewhat indigestible and will regurgitate after a few days. Feed stewing beef, but never hamburger.

Now to the important aspect of method of feeding stock. It is of no use to merely drop pieces of fish into a cage housing a number of snakes. This will inevitably result in several snakes seizing the same piece of fish, and the wild thrashing about can mean possible jaw injuries or even accidental cannibalism if snakes of different sizes are involved. At best the disturbance will

18

probably result in specimens which do not feed readily being put off feeding for some while. The writer's method has been to individually feed each snake. Although this might seem a daunting prospect if one has upwards of one hundred specimens to attend to, in practice the process can be quick. Adult snakes are fed weekly and young specimens up to around fifteen inches long twice weekly. The system is to have all the food cut up ready, and several empty cages or small plastic cans with lids on hand. Wash your hands thoroughly and rub on a little lemon juice to remove the smell of fish. A hungry snake that knows food is in the offering, will bite at anything that smells of fish. The first snake is lifted out by hand, given a suitably sized piece of food (it is advisable to hold the food in forceps as a hungry snake will strike indiscriminantly at food or fingers), and placed immediately in an empty cage or can. Whilst it is swallowing the food the next snake is being fed and placed in the second empty cage. By the time the third snake is taking its food the first specimen fed will have swallowed its meal and can be returned to its original cage. By working this on a rota system, it is surprising how many snakes can be fed in a short period of time. An added advantage with this individual feeding is that if a snake is off its food and possibly sickly it is noticed quickly, and the specimen can be isolated from other stock in case of infection.

It has been found with snakes born and reared under captive conditions that they are quite eager to accept food whilst being handled. Newly purchased adult stock may not be so accommodating, and here it will be necessary to "tease" them with a piece of fish held in forceps, until they snap at the food. After taking one or two meals in this way they usually settle down enough to feed whilst being handled.

Note:- For details of composition of "Abidec" multivitamin preparation, see Appendix 5.

19

5. BREEDING — GENERAL COMMENTS

The breeding of captive reptiles, even in large zoological institutions, is the exception rather than the rule. This appears to be mainly due to the disturbance of various physiological rhythms and season "timetables" which stimulate such activities as courtship and mating. The effect of light, humidity and temperature upon reptilian behaviour is still not completely understood. What has become very apparent to the author is that the rate of success with breeding from snakes which have had a few years in the wild (that is, captured when adult), compares very unfavorably with results from specimens born and brought to maturity in captivity. A wild-caught gravid female garter snake will produce her young with little trouble, but captive conditions will usually inhibit subsequent courting and mating behaviour. It seems that once the seasonal rhythm to which the snake has been accustomed is broken (and here one of the main factors is hibernation in the winter months), then a female will not be receptive to coition however ardent the behaviour of a male companion.

Hibernation is not easy to arrange unless one has access to an outdoor enclosure where the snakes can take their winter rest in semi-natural conditions, far enough below ground level to be safe from frost. To try to reproduce the conditions necessary indoors (that is, in a cool basement or garage) almost always results in the creatures not being cold enough for complete hibernation. Stores of body fat are used up much too quickly, and if they manage to survive until the spring they will be in such a weak and emaciated state as to be useless for any breeding program, which of course requires healthy and vigorous snakes.

The writer's system with wild-caught adult females (on the very few times success was achieved) was to pack them away in hibernation for a period of four to six weeks only. Boxes containing newspapers, dry leaves and hay were used, and kept in a cool garage. After the time had expired, the snakes were gradually brought back to active life, and after three weeks or so introduced to a male snake. Successful matings occurred, and the conclusion that can perhaps be drawn from this is that as far as the metabolism of the female snakes was concerned, the hibernation had been completed and the next activity was the normal spring mating period.

If one wishes to allow stock to hibernate every winter and has satisfactory facilities to allow for this in outdoor enclosures, then there is certainly no objection to the procedure. The snakes can live a semi-natural existence, and mating, deposition of young and hibernation will occur at the normal times in their annual cycle, dependent on the climate where the herpetologist happens to reside. The main disadvantage with this arrangement is the resultant lack of control over the inhabitants' behaviour. It is difficult, if not impossible, to keep accurate records of matings, gestation periods and births of litters if these activities can occur regularly without one's knowledge. By the time the birth of a litter is discovered the chance of saving any weak specimens may have been long gone. Feeding can also be a problem as the snakes will need to be fed in daylight hours when the weather and prevailing temperature is suitable. In all probability this will not coincide with one's available spare time. Under controlled indoor conditions feeding programmes can be implemented whenever spare time permits, regardless of time of day or night. When there are large numbers of snakes to be fed this can be very important.

6. MATINGS

To begin with it would be as well to outline briefly the typical courtship and mating behaviour of garter snakes, which is a fairly standardized performance common (with certain exceptions) to most of the non-venomous Colubrid snakes. It begins with the male approaching the female and rubbing his chin along her back, and at the same time matching the contours of her body with his own. He may travel up and down the female's back a number of times before taking up a position parallel to the female with his vent close to hers. Spasmodic muscular rippling movements then pass like waves forward from his tail to his head, and if conditions are right this usually stimulates the female to allow coupling. The female's role is one of passive acceptance of the male, although rarely she can make the initial advances (see Appendix 3). A loop of the male's body is then pushed under the female to bring her tail up and allow the penetration of one hemipenis. This manoeuvre is carried out extremely quickly, and even if one is watching closely it is only possible to see a blur of movement and then observe that the snakes are joined at the vent. Coupling may occur after only brief preliminary courtship, or may be a prolonged procedure. If the female refuses to mate the male will eventually lose interest and leave her, although matings have been witnessed after almost two hours of concentrated attention by a male. The snakes can remain coupled for as little as ten minutes (anything less than this is unlikely to prove fruitful) or for as long as several hours.

Newly born Garter Snakes *(Thamnophis sirtalis sirtalis)* about to emerge from their membranous sacs.

The same snakes a few hours later.

The convulsive waves along the male's body usually cease once union is established, but in a considerable number of matings observed of the Mountain garter snake (*Thamnophis elegans elegans*) the actions continued for some time. On several occasions the female coiled like a watchspring with the male coiled similarly above her, caressing her with the wave-like movements. This then is the performance to expect if both snakes are ready for mating. Adults of both sexes can be housed together, and then if conditions and inclinations are right matings can take place. This advantage may be outweighed by the fact that such actions are likely to be unobserved, and thus no notes can be made. One can never be sure, if numbers of snakes are kept together, whether a particular snake is sterile or has just not mated. As in other animals, some individuals are better breeders than others, and if one is aware which specimens are the best breeding stock and which are virtually non-breeders, then time and effort can be saved in housing and feeding snakes which are almost certain to be unproductive.

I am in favour of keeping the sexes separately caged, and arranging regular introductions in the hope that matings will take place while the specimens are under observation. A male that is particularly ardent can be tried with several females until one that is willing to mate is located. It has been known for an Eastern garter snake to mate with three females one after the other, and for litters to result from each union. From the writer's own records there are details of a young male Mountain garter snake which mated on the 15th, 23rd and 31st of December with three females from the same litter as himself, resulting in three litters being born toward the end of the following April.

The best time to introduce a male snake into a female's cage is immediately after she has shed. For a brief while the female's skin is damp after she is free from the old epidermis, and the smell of this fluid which serves to assist in the separation of the old and new skins appears to excite a male snake and induce frantic courting activity. To a lesser extent a male is liable to be stimulated into sexual activity if he has himself shed. Yet the successful introductions which result in matings are largely a matter of trial and error. Sometimes one notices a certain restlessness on the part of a female and an ultrasensitivity to being handled which shows itself in a barely discernible jerkiness of movement. This may mean that she is ready for mating.

Wild-caught specimens are most likely to breed in early spring.

Under controlled conditions indoors with specimens reared from birth the time of year has little or no effect on the mating impulse. As soon as the snakes are sexually mature they are ready for the introductions; sexual maturity depends on size, not age. There is a very interesting paper by Charles C. Carpenter on Garter snakes in Michigan (see Further Reading) where it is shown that males can reach maturity in their second spring before they are two years old, and some two-year-old females can produce young. It all depends on whether they been able to put on sufficient growth. Of course, these observations are based on snakes which are subject to a normal hibernation period, and growth is limited to approximately five months of the year, May through September, there being no significant growth outside this period. With snakes under the artificial conditions already discussed growth is continuous, and maturity is reached in a comparatively short time.

With Garter snakes (disregarding certain dwarf species) a male is capable of mating by the time it is eighteen to nineteen inches in length. At around the twenty-two to twenty-four inch mark a female can produce young. There are, no doubt, exceptions to these lengths, but this is merely a guide to the appropriate time to consider breeding from young stock.

Matings can take place at any time in the year under artificial conditions, and this is of great benefit to the snake breeder. These snakes normally mate in April and early May, and deposit young in July through September. With a large stock of snakes producing young at the same period it would be extremely difficult to cope with the flood of youngsters, whereas with litters arriving at all months of the year the business of attending to the babies at the time they need the most care is much easier.

Before leaving the subject of mating a word is advisable on a point which might worry someone who has not previously witnessed snake coupling. After snakes have been in coition for a

San Francisco Garter Snake *(Thamnophis sirtalis tetrataenia)* Adult female.

certain time, and the female wishes to free herself from the male, the action taken can be extremely violent, and to an observer almost certain to result in permanent injury to the male. In view of the structure of the hemipenis, which when erect is virtually inside-out and securing a hold inside the female by means of spines, he is unable to withdraw quickly, and has to wait until the organ resumes its normal size before this can be accomplished. A female tends to drag the male backwards, and he is forced to follow her every movement. If merely moving along fails to free her the female can resort to violent body rolling, twisting the male around all the time. It is as well to have little in the way of cage furnishings, since a female can roll into, say, a clump of grass, which allows her to exert a tremendous pull on the male, who, because of the obstructions, cannot follow her movements easily. The snakes will eventually part, and it appears rare for a male to suffer damage from such an encounter.

It must be appreciated that not all matings will result in successful fertilization of eggs. If, after four weeks, it is not possible, by allowing a female to glide through one's fingers, to feel by gentle pressure a series of small lumps then it can be safely assumed that another mating is necessary. The lumps will be more obvious toward the vent, and particularly noticeable in the reasonably narrow-bodied Garter snake. It is not quite so easy with female Water snakes in view of their bulk, but if one lets the snake slide through the hand keeping the thumb on top with index and middle fingers exerting light pressure underneath it should be possible to be aware of a soft lumpy mass. The secret is to let the snake move slowly and somewhat limply. If it is struggling to escape then the body will be tense and the body-wall muscles taut, making it difficult to form any opinion as to the snake's condition.

7. GESTATION PERIOD

The period of gestation depends to a large extent on the temperature at which gravid snakes are kept, the period being accelerated by heat. Two American experts, F. N. and F. C. Blanchard, carried out a great deal of research on the Eastern garter snake and they estimated that the date of birth could be brought forward four and a half days earlier by each degree Centigrade increase in the average temperature during gestation. They also found that the period with this snake can vary from eighty-seven days in an exceptionally hot summer, to one-hundred and sixteen days in an unusually cold one.

Under the conditions described in the first chapter most Eastern garters have given birth after ninety to one-hundred days. The Western variety (Mountain garter snake) tends to have a longer period, usually around one-hundred and twenty-five days. The longest period encountered for this species was one hundred and fifty days, but this resulted in only one living baby, the remainder being still-born.

Water snakes (*Natrix sipedon subspecies*) normally took between one-hundred and seven and one-hundred and twenty-five days, although a number of much longer pregnancies resulted in healthy litters.

It is best to work on the basis of the shortest possible period, and give the gravid female special treatment from then on until the litter is deposited. During the early part of the gestation period the temperatures can be kept reasonably high all the time, but when the anticipated birth date is getting near it is definitely advisable to vary the temperatures, that is, let the female have a regular "cooling off" period. This is logical when you consider that in the wild state, the baby snakes are born in late summer and early fall, when there is a distinct drop in temperature at night. This variation in temperature may well be the necessary trigger which prompts the female into giving birth. It is the author's opinion that constant high temperatures may cause the female to refrain from giving birth to her litter at the correct time, retaining the young until they are dead and perhaps even decomposing before depositing them. The added danger in this situation is that the decomposed remains of one or two babies may be permanently retained in the body forming hard lumps. Such blockages may or may not affect the general health of the snake but will probably make the specimen useless for further breeding.

When the estimated birth date is near the female snake should be caged alone, and be undisturbed as far as is possible. She has quite probably refused food for some weeks, but this should not cause alarm as she will certainly recommence feeding immediately the litter is deposited.

The cage should have a quantity of sphagnum moss on the floor, and in one end of the cage it should be kept damp. A few extra pieces of cork bark can also be introduced.

Although it may easily pass unnoticed, a sign that the birth of young is imminent is in the restless behaviour of the female. She will sometimes keep on the move exploring every corner of the cage for anything up to forty-eight hours before the event.

This behaviour is much more readily apparent in egg-laying snakes. Even though suitable locations to deposit eggs are available, a female may nevertheless move around pushing her head into corners in an endless search, presumably, for an even better situation. This activity is sometimes so prolonged and persistent that the snake's snout is rubbed raw.

Snakes are not any more susceptible to disease during the gestation period. Special treatment is really limited to keeping handling down to the minimum, and caging the female alone toward the end of the pregnancy. If, however, before this time it is noticed that the activity of other snakes is causing annoyance to the female, or there is the chance of heavy companions lying on her, then she should be put in solitary confinement earlier.

Immediately after the birth of young (or in the case of egg-layers, deposition of the clutch) the female snake normally presents a sorry appearance with stretched skin hanging in folds, and she may well be limp and weak after her efforts. She should be left as far as possible undisturbed for a while, although some specimens are very eager for food straightaway. It is a good plan to make a dish of warm water available as a good soak is sometimes appreciated. Recovery of normal appearance and strength is surprisingly rapid.

Every effort should be made to ensure that a gravid snake is free from external parasites before a litter is born. In particular if mites are present, it is possible for some to be picked up by the babies even if the litter is removed to a separate cage soon after birth. These parasites are a serious enough problem on adult snakes, but on diminuitive newly-born specimens they can become fatal rapidly. Quite apart from the severe degree of torment to such tiny creatures, a large number of mites can quickly extract a dangerous quantity of blood. In the unfortunate event of a mite infestation involving baby snakes immediate measures should be taken, using the Shell "No-Pest" strip (Vapona) as detailed previously.

8. BIRTH OF YOUNG

If one is lucky enough to be able to witness the birth of a litter of snakes, it is not only a fascinating experience but also means that one is on hand to remove the young fairly quickly, and obviate the danger of them being damaged or killed by the heavy body of the female in the confines of a small cage. The addition of sphagnum moss and pieces of cork bark is to provide retreats for the newly born young in the event of the birth not being discovered for some hours. Although a female will certainly not go out of her way to damage the babies there is always the chance she will accidentally lie on a few and suffocate them. The larger the snake, the greater the chance.

The birth process starts as a series of contractions along the latter half of the female's body. These contractions are much easier to observe in a Garter snake than in the thicker bodied Water snake. The effect is as if a piece of string looped around the body had been pulled tight and then quickly relaxed. At this stage the female should on no account be disturbed, and any observations should be carried out discretely and quietly. Once the young ones start to emerge there is usually at least a five minute interval between them, sometimes much longer.

The babies are contained in transparent membranes which normally rupture soon after birth (following thrusting movements by the babies to force their heads through), although sometimes this occurs during or immediately before birth. Survival chances seem highest for those babies which emerge from their enclosing membranes soon after deposition. Most of the

31

Newborn Mountain Garter Snakes (*Thamnophis elegans elegans*)

babies which emerge before or during actual birth are considerably weakened and soon die. Some may in fact be already dead before they are free of the female. This is possibly because they do not have the benefit of the "cushioning" effect of the membrane which contains a certain amount of fluid.

If the sacs are intact it is best to quietly remove them to another cage of damp sphagnum moss.

As already indicated, the babies emerge from the membranes by merely pushing their heads through. There is no need for them to cut a way through a leathery eggshell by means of an eggtooth. They do not seem to need a prolonged rest once they commence breathing, and are usually quite mobile within a few minutes. This is in complete contrast to the babies of egg-laying species, which after the strenuous business of cutting through tough eggshells, normally rest (sometimes for many hours) with only heads protruding as if reluctant to leave, even withdrawing back into the egg if disturbed.

If the babies have been deposited at the right time, their first move after emerging from the membranes should be to slough their skins. This is the reason for the damp moss in the cage; to assist this activity by keeping the conditions humid. It has to be borne in mind that these little snakes are but six to eight inches long, and at this stage of their existence do not have great reserves of energy. It must be made as easy as possible for them to slough, otherwise the epidermis will harden and have the effect of encasing the little snakes in stiff leathery overcoats. Snake keepers will know that it is possible to manually assist a snake in this condition to slough by peeling the old skin off with forceps or fingers, after the specimen has been soaked in warm water. Although this can be highly successful with sizeable specimens it is a different matter altogether with slender fragile six-inch snakelets. Every effort should therefore be made to provide the babies with conditions which make it easy for them to cast unassisted and in a natural manner.

Occasionally a litter is deposited a little early, and the young will have opaque eyes indicating that they will not be sloughing for several days. In this case merely make sure they are able to clean all traces of sticky fluid from their bodies. This they can normally accomplish easily by crawling through the damp moss provided. It is advisable to keep part of their cage damp until sloughing takes place.

After the female has deposited all her young, she will pres-

Newly hatched Viperine Snakes (*Natrix maura*) .

ent a somewhat emaciated appearance, with deep folds of loose skin along her body.

As she has probably refused food for some weeks prior to the birth of her litter it is in order to separate her and offer food straight-away, and within a day or so she will have "regained her figure".

It would appear that a female garter snake needs at least a five-month break between the birth of a litter and a subsequent mating. The few matings which occurred in less than this period of time did not prove productive. It would seem that this rest period also applies to the water snakes, although on one occasion the mating of a pair of Broadbanded water snakes just over three months after parturition proved successful, and another litter resulted.

Deformed hatchling Viperine Snake. Although having gone full term, this baby snake was unable to emerge from the egg because of the kinks and distorted body. Specimens like this should be preserved for further study.

9. CARE OF BABY SNAKES

For the first couple of days after birth it is best to leave the babies undisturbed. This is of course, once it is certain that each one has shed satisfactorily. Sometimes in a litter there are one or two babies with marked deformities, such as kinks in the backbone or coiled and stumpy tails. Such specimens may not be worth rearing but should not be discarded out of hand. They could provide useful material for an embryologist or someone doing research into reptile abnormalities, and should therefore be euthanised with chloroform and then placed in a jar of 5 per cent formalin for preservation.

The first step in rearing the babies, whether garter or water snakes, is to get them to accept their first meal. If a supply of very small fish (unwanted substandard tropical fish from a breeder are ideal) is available no problem arises. If the season is right frog or toad tadpoles are a good food. If this live food is available it can be left in the cage in a water dish of suitable size, and a good proportion of the baby snakes will start feeding. If live food is not available then other methods are necessary. With garter snakes other than the western varieties the first meal offered can be earthworms. Once a young snake has taken an earthworm it can be offered a small piece of raw fish, and if this is taken there is normally no trouble with future meals. Raw fish will be readily accepted without the earthworm "appetizer".

Do not leave earthworms in a cage of young snakes as it is very easy for two snakes to grab opposite ends of the same worm, and for one of them to attempt to swallow its companion. This can result in suffocation for both of them. Care should be taken not to use the brightly banded worms (known in Britain as "brandlings") found in rotting vegetation, as these contain substances which are distasteful, and perhaps even poisonous, to small snakes.

With western garter snakes and water snakes that cannot be started off with earthworms, it is possible usually to tease a few specimens into taking a piece of raw fish flesh. Holding the fish in forceps, the snake's head is gently tapped with it near the mouth. Water snakes in particular will be inclined to snap in annoyance. Once they have bitten the fish one must keep perfectly still, and the chances are that the food will be swallowed. Some youngsters will not respond to this treatment in that although the food is snapped at it is only held in the jaws for a few seconds, and then rejected. For them it will be necessary to tease them with a small whole fish or perhaps a frog limb. Persuading the little snakes to take their first meal is the troublesome task; after this they should accept any food smelling even slightly fishy.

Baby snakes should be fed, as much as they will take eagerly, twice a week. Their cage should be kept quite dry with only a small water dish. Baby snakes are likely to crawl into their water dish and drown themselves. They should be examined regularly when they are fed, to see if any of them are having difficulty in shedding. Any found in this condition can be put in a separate cage of damp moss until shedding is completed.

Growth should be fairly rapid, and within a couple of months it will be necessary to reduce the number of snakes to each cage. Shedding should be fairly regular. If the babies are feeding well it should occur approximately every four weeks. Once a snake is mature sloughing occurs at more infrequent intervals.

It should be possible to sex the baby snakes by examination of the shape and general outline of the tail (see diagram). Although some herpetologists seem to have difficulty in sexing other than sexually mature snakes, the author has found that the tail shape differences apply (although perhaps to a lesser extent) in juvenile specimens, and this method can be used with almost one hundred per cent accuracy. Early sex determination can be very useful because obviously one wishes to raise more females than males, and so build up a good breeding stock.

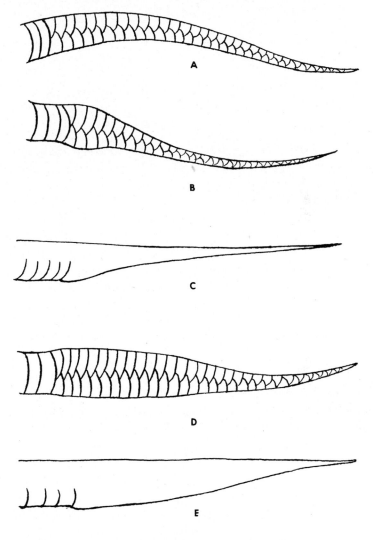

A, B, & C. - Female Tail; ventral and lateral views. The tail base enlargement noticeable in some females (see B) appear to be male glands, but note that the tail tapers rapidly.

D & E. - Male Tail; ventral and lateral views. Tail base is thick, and this thickness extends for some distance beyond the vent.

10. NOTES ON EGG INCUBATION

The herpetologist will no doubt wish to breed snakes other than Garter and Water snakes and extend his activities to include the egg-laying species, which far outnumber the livebearers in the snake world. To successfully incubate snake eggs is not just a matter of keeping the eggs warm as one would with chicken eggs. The parchment-like or leathery shell of the snake egg is very porous, and the main problem in incubation is providing the correct humidity in addition to the right temperature. If the eggs are kept too dry then they shrivel and the embryo within dies. If kept too wet the growth of fungus is encouraged and the end result is the same — a dead embryo. The correct humidity is that which allows the eggs to remain full and rounded without being actually wet.

Taking things in their logical sequence the first item for consideration is getting the snakes to mate. Here the comments made already in a previous chapter relating to Garter and Water snakes apply equally well to Corn, Rat, King and other American egg-laying snakes (and the European relatives of the Water snakes (*Natrix*), which are all egg-layers). Experiments are necessary to trigger off the courtship and mating, and the snakes should be introduced to each other at different times, different temperatures and in different surroundings, etc., until mating is achieved.

Once it is obvious the female snake is gravid, and eggs can be clearly seen or felt in her body she should be caged alone. It is essential at this time to have one end of the cage damp, and the most convenient way is to use a clump of damp sphagnum moss. This could, perhaps, be covered by a large piece of cork bark. Unlike the livebearers, the snake can be kept at 75 to 85 degrees F. all the time as there seems to be no advantage gained by dropping the temperature at night. In fact, there is evidence to suggest that with regard to the European Natrix continued low temperatures at the time the female is carrying the eggs can result in the delay of oviposition, allowing the eggs to increase in size until they are too large to be laid. An eggbound snake is not a pretty sight as the size of the eggs causes the skin to become tightly distended over each one of them. There is little to be done for a snake in this condition, as it is usually lethargic and unable to feed, and even if it is then kept warm it cannot deposit the oversized eggs, and death results. The author has also encountered this egg-binding problem when trying to breed the European Sand lizard (*Lacerta agilis*).

The snake will, in all probability, lay her eggs in the damp part of the cage. Check daily and remove them for incubation before they have commenced to dehydrate. Be especially careful when removing the eggs from the cage. If they have stuck together, **do not** attempt to separate them. To do so will surely break the shells of the eggs and kill the babies within. If any eggs are found to be badly dehydrated, do not discard these but bury them in damp sand for about twenty-four hours. If they have filled out after this time there is a good chance they have been saved. It is also wise however, to place them in a separate incubator and closely watch them for signs of collapse or fungus, which could indicate that the embryos are in fact dead.

Individual herpetologists and zoological institutions usually have their own 'pet' method of incubating reptile eggs, and the writer is well aware that other methods than his own are probably just as successful.

Appendix 4 details the method used for the incubation of the eggs of the Everglades Rat snake (*Elaphe obsoleta rossalleni*). Here the incubation media was damp paper tissues in small plastic containers. Some difficulties were experienced with several of the eggs when the shells developed deep indentations indicating they were starting to dry out, but this was remedied by burying them in damp sand for a period until they had absorbed enough moisture to become full and round again. St. Louis Zoological Park has had a great deal of success with hatching reptile eggs by using peat moss as the incubation material. This has water added to it and is then kneaded into a damp but still friable texture with the hands. Eggs are placed in this media inside plastic bags, which are not then opened unless the incubation period exceeds sixty days. The eggs can, of course, be observed without being disturbed. The only thing to bear in mind when using plastic bags instead of containers, is that the hatchling snake's very efficient egg-tooth, which enables it to slice through the leathery egg shell, can also be used, just as efficiently, to cut a way out of the plastic bag. Make sure, therefore, that the bags are contained in an 'escape-proof' container of some kind.

Sand is a good media and has been used with success with lizard eggs and also with clutches from various species of European Natrix (English Grass snake — *Natrix natrix helvetica*, Italian or Two-striped Grass snake — *Natrix natrix natrix*, Dice or Tessellated snake — *Natrix tessellata* and the Viperine snake — *Natrix maura*). The disadvantage however, is that the eggs cannot be examined without digging them out of the sand. There is a greater chance of them becoming too wet and virtually waterlogged, and the first indication of this is the appearance of a fine growth of mould. If sand is used it should be well washed (preferably boiled) beforehand. If mould does appear, it is most unlikely that any eggs will hatch.

Media such as damp sphagnum moss or sawdust, although used in some quarters with success, are not really suitable as the aim should be to keep the eggs in reasonably sterile surroundings. For this reason the author now prefers to use damp paper tissues. Eggs are merely placed on top of several layers of tissues and covered with one tissue. The containers used have been anything from aluminum biscuit tins to glass jam jars, but the plastic food containers with snap-on lids now readily obtainable are ideal incubators.

The best temperature at which to keep eggs would appear to be in the region of 80 to 85 degrees Fahrenheit. Temperatures much higher than this are not advisable, as although the writer has seen a report of Viperine snake (*Natrix maura*) eggs being incubated at 95 degrees (plus or minus 2 degrees), there seems to be a possibility of malformation or even death to embryos subjected to excessive heat.

The period of incubation varies with each species of snake. At the temperature recommended the eggs of European Water snakes (*Natrix*) should hatch after approximately forty-five days. A large clutch of Grass snake (*Natrix natrix helvetica*) eggs incubated in 1960 hatched in forty-one to fifty days. Eggs of the larger snakes, such as the Rat snakes (Elaphe) need around seventy days incubation.

A note should be kept of the estimated date of hatching for any clutch of eggs under incubation. Normally the first signs one notices of an impending hatching is the presence of frothy liquid emanating from a small slit on the egg. If one is lucky it will be possible to observe the young snake making further slits with its eggtooth, until it is able to protrude its head and take its first breath. If unduly disturbed at this point it will immediately retract. Complete emergence may not take place for some hours, perhaps not until the following day, but do not be tempted to assist the babies out of their shells. The babies do not cast their first skins until one or two weeks has passed after hatching, and it is usually wasted effort to offer them food before this takes place. Most of them will, in any case, be quite plump with the unabsorbed yolk still present in their bodies.

Some literature on the general subject of reptile eggs seems to indicate that eggs must on no account be rotated, but must be incubated in the same position in which they were laid. This is done by marking the top of the eggs with ink when they are discovered, and depositing them in the incubation media with the mark still on top, being careful not to revolve them during the moving process. This may be necessary for turtle or crocodilian eggs; the writer has no practical experience with these so he is not in a position to form an opinion. With snake eggs, however, rotation of the eggs, although possibly not advisable, need not have a deleterious effect on their development. An extreme example can be quoted. A small clutch of eggs of the Italian Grass snake (*Natrix natrix natrix* — two-striped color phase) was discovered by a friend in a pet store and sent by ordinary mail to the writer. Most of the eggs were considerably dehydrated (and apparently infertile) on arrival, but two good ones were incubated in damp sand and hatched successfully. These eggs must have been rotated many hundreds of times during their seventeen hours of travel through the mail, but still with no ill effects on the embryos.

11. SUMMARY OF BREEDING EXPERIMENTS
- GARTER SNAKES

The first encounter with Garter snakes was in 1957, when a gravid female was purchased from a dealer. The experiences with attempting to rear the babies and breeding from them formed the subject of the article in Appendix 1. Discouraged by the fact that it only seemed possible to raise a couple of specimens from each litter interest waned, and the stock was sold.

In 1964 another gravid female Eastern Garter snake was purchased, and this gave birth to twelve rather puny young ones late in August. Seven of these were kept and reared to maturity and there were high hopes of breeding from them.

This started a serious interest in the problems of breeding snakes under captive conditions, and all available literature was read in an attempt to find some relevant information. The various papers by the Blanchards seemed to be the only detailed accounts of Garter snake breeding, and provided much useful food for thought. However, they referred to breeding the creatures in outdoor enclosures, where the snakes were subject to prevailing weather conditions and, in fact, lived a semi-natural existence. What was in mind was the possibility of breeding snakes under strictly controlled and completely unnatural conditions indoors, but certain of the Blanchards' observations relating to gravid females brought indoors were not encouraging. They commented that this resulted in abnormal broods, often dead at birth, and born over a period of days or weeks.

Also being considered at this time was the possible crossbreeding of different varieties of Garter and perhaps Water snakes. Private correspondence with Professor Charles C. Carpenter of the University of Oklahoma was extremely helpful as he succinctly explained the differences between hybrids and intergrades. An extract from one of his letters reads as follows:-

"By definition, the concept of subspecies implies that interbreeding between subspecies is to be expected — the progenies of such crosses are called intergrades. Subspecies occupy separate geographical ranges and natural intergrades often occur in areas where the ranges come together.

The concept of species implies that they generally do not or cannot interbreed. If progenies do result from crosses between two different species, they are usually infertile and they are called hybrids. Species of the same genus can and do often occupy overlapping geographical ranges. Thus, subspecies of *Thamnophis* belonging to the same species could interbreed, but the chances of two different species of the same genus, whether *Thamnophis* or *Natrix*, interbreeding is quite remote, though not impossible. Both *Natrix erythrogaster* and *Natrix sipedon* are found in Oklahoma, but I know of no hybrids.

The reasons why they do not cross (isolating mechanisms) could be due to a number of different causes — behavioural, chromosomal, structural, chemical, etc.

Eastern and western subspecies of the same species could be expected to crossbreed and produce viable young."

In August 1965 a gravid female Mountain Garter snake (*Thamnophis elegans elegans*) was purchased, and this soon gave birth to twelve sturdy youngsters. At this time the multivitamin preparation "Abidec" was being used in the snakes' drinking water, and the growth of the young Mountain Garter snakes reflected the importance of such a supplement. The growth was, in fact, so rapid that the largest female produced a litter before she was twelve months old (see Appendix 2).

Meanwhile, attempts were being made to get the Eastern Garter snakes (born 1964) to mate. The Blanchards had arranged matings in their outdoor pits almost solely in the month of April, indicating that if the snakes did not mate within a certain period after the onset of warm spring weather then the inclination to mate evaporated, and the snakes became indifferent to each other's presence. The Eastern Garter snakes were left in an out-

44

door horticultural-frame type of enclosure for several days at the end of April, but the male showed absolutely no interest at all in the female. These snakes had not had the benefit of the vitamin addition to their diet for the first year of their lives, and lacked the vitality of the snakes that had received this supplement from birth. Any breeding plans for these particular Eastern Garter snakes were discontinued. This disappointing spring attempt at an outdoor mating happened a couple of months before the early mating of the Mountain Garter snakes, which took place indoors in a small cage. This first indoor mating gave encouragement for the future, and in the ensuing years many litters of Mountain Garter snakes were born. One of the early problems was with the retention of young by the females resulting in them being born dead. It was later discovered that variation in cage temperatures for the female in the later stages of her pregnancy helped to avoid this. Even in litters which contained living young there was a disappointingly high incidence of babies which had gone full term only to die shortly before birth.

Details of a series of matings and subsequent births relating to the Mountain Garter snake may be of interest, and diary extracts are now given. It must be borne in mind that the particular species in question does not have the sometimes enormous litters associated occasionally with the Eastern Garter snake, the average being around eight to ten (lowest recorded, two: highest, seventeen).

All snakes were given a coding for identification, specimens being recognized by distinctive color or scaling irregularities.

IDENTIFICATION CODINGS

T.e.e.65B/M.01 - Largest male with orange venter.

T.e.e.65B/M.02 - Smaller male with yellowish venter.

T.e.e.65B/F.03 - Largest female with brightest dorsal stripe, and lacking tail-tip.

T.e.e.65B/F.04 - Female with divided ventral scales preceding vent.

T.e.e.65B/F.05 - Female with extra small pre-vent scale.

T.e.e.65B/F.06 - Darkest female with grey dorsal stripes.

T.e.e.65B/F.07 - Female with scarred ventral scale close to head.

(These codings are constructed by first taking the name of the subspecies, that is *Thamnophis elegans elegans* equals T.e.e. Then follows the year of acquisition, and B or P, which denotes born in the collection or purchased. Finally, M or F for male or female, and the particular specimen's code number.)

MATINGS - DECEMBER 1966.

MATING NO. 1. 15th. DECEMBER -
T.e.e.65B/M.01 X T.e.e.65B/F.06

Male introduced to female 9:15 p.m. Mating almost immediate with little courting activity. Continued convulsive waves after union achieved. Female passive until 10:25 p.m. when she began struggling and rolling violently - male dragged over and over. Still in coition at 11:25 p.m. Not observed again until 7:30 a.m. next morning. Union over 2 hours 10 mins. Lumps felt in female's body on 23rd. December.

MATING NO. 2. 15th. DECEMBER -
T.e.e.65B/M.02 X T.e.e.65B/F.04

Union at 9:30 p.m. after fifteen minutes courting. At 10:40 p.m. female was passive and coiled like a watchspring, with male outside still caressing her with convulsive waves. At 10:47 p.m. violent body rolling by female. Not observed again until next morning. Coition over 1 hour 55 min. Lumps felt in female's body 31st. December.

MATING NO. 3. 17th. DECEMBER -
T.e.e.65B/M.02 X T.e.e.65B/F.07

Male introduced at 2:15 p.m. Union immediate. Female started body rolling forty minutes later, which made the male more ardent with convulsive waves passing vigorously along his body. Parted sometime between 4:30 p.m. and 5:00 p.m. Coition over 2 hours 15 mins.

MATING NO. 4. 23rd. DECEMBER -
T.e.e.65B/M.01 X T.e.e.65B/F.05

Courting for approximately thirty minutes before coupling (male introduced 1:30 p.m.) Female passive until 2:30 p.m. then body rolling and writhing. Extremely violent rolling at 4:10 p.m. after which snakes parted. Length of coition 2 hours 10 mins. Lumps evident in female's body in latter part of January.

MATING NO. 5. 31st. DECEMBER -
T.e.e.65B/M.01 X T.e.e.65B/F.03

Female caged with male immediately after she had cast skin. Male started courting straightaway but female would not respond. Union achieved at 1:10 p.m. after almost two hours of activity by the male. At 3:15 p.m. female started struggling, moving quickly around the cage dragging the male after her. Violent body rolling at 3:45 p.m., and snakes parted five minutes later. Coition 2 hours 40 mins. Lumps in female not evident until beginning of February. Size increased rapidly after this time, and within a few weeks she was the thickest of pregnant females.

BIRTHS

FROM MATING NO. 1.

Young produced 22 APRIL 1967 (Gestation period 128 days). No living babies. Four hard masses containing decomposed snakes (two not fully developed) and one large yolk mass.

FROM MATING NO. 2.

Young produced 8 APRIL 1967 (Gestation period 114 days). Five living young and one stillborn. One very dark baby died an hour after birth. Four survivors believed to be two males and two females.

FROM MATING NO. 3.

Young produced 22 APRIL 1967 (Gestation period 126 days). Early morning female observed moving around dragging a partly emerged (and dead) baby. Large yolky mass found in cage. Another mass deposited at 1:00 p.m., and at 2:00 p.m. a hard mass containing a decomposed embryo. On the 29 April, seven days later, the female deposited one fully developed dead baby, and two yolky lumps.

FROM MATING NO. 4.

Young produced 27 APRIL 1967 (Gestation period 125 days). Six babies born, three of them dead.

FROM MATING NO. 5.

Young produced 30 APRIL 1967 (Gestation period 120 days). First baby born 7:00 p.m. Eight born, four of them dead (these appeared to have emerged from their membranes inside the

47

female). One of four living was very weak — took one breath only. Eyedropper used to pump air into lungs and baby apparently shocked into resuming breathing. After an hour baby snake broke away from yolk sac. In this litter was a reddish marked male — the brightest specimen from any litter.

Total number of living young from five litters — eleven.

The number of young saved in relation to the litters born was not too good, but these were the early days of gathering information and trying to understand the conditions necessary for successful breeding. This particular subspecies seemed more prone than others to still-births, but nevertheless the numbers in the collection rose and eventually it was necessary to select only the best snakes and find means to dispose of the surplus.

In the summer of 1966 a very large gravid Garter snake was obtained from a Dutch livestock dealer (who had been requested to reserve any obviously gravid specimens received in consignments from the United States). This was a Two-striped Garter snake (*Thamnophis couchi hammondi*) which was in a very poor condition, and it had some injury to the neck, causing it to hold its head to one side, and with most of the tail missing. It was hoped, however, to keep it alive long enough for the litter to be produced. It was kept under observation and was seen to be having contractions preparatory to giving birth, but it was apparently too weak to expel the young. The snake's condition rapidly deteriorated over a period of a few hours until breathing ceased. There were still slight muscular responses from the tail stump so in case there was still a flicker of life the brain was quickly destroyed. The belly was opened and thirty-six young ones removed. They were all fully developed but with opaque eyes, indicating that in all probability they had been within a couple of days of birth. The problem then was whether to remove them forcibly from their transparent sacs, or keep them moist for a couple of days and allow them to emerge from the membranes unaided. Six specimens were released but they appeared very weak and unable to make other than uncontrolled wriggling movements. It was decided to keep the remaining thirty moist and leave them to their own devices, but as it happened this was the wrong decision. All thirty young died without attempting to emerge, but the six

48

released babies survived (after careful "nursing") and lived to produce litters of their own.

Apart from the litters that were being produced by specimens born and raised in the collection, a standing order was kept with the Dutch dealer for any gravid females. Although as a rule almost all the babies from such females were not kept, it was felt that every possible opportunity should be taken to observe the behavior of females and the births of as many litters as possible to gain information.

In 1968 amongst several gravid females received were two typical examples of the Eastern Garter snake which gave birth to litters including several all black (melanistic) babies. Three black young appeared in a litter of twenty-six, and four in a litter of eight. This was indeed a pleasant surprise as melanism only occurs in certain isolated areas in the wild, and specimens (rarely available) commanded a high price compared with normal striped Garter snakes. Once again a paper of the Blanchards proved helpful (see Furthur Reading). They had shown that the factor for melanism was a normal Mendelian recessive factor. The implications of this, insofar as it affects snake breeding are discussed in Chapter 13. All the black babies were raised and, in fact, the largest male was mated back to his mother in 1970, resulting in a litter of eighteen young, eleven of these living (six black; five striped) and seven dead (four black; three striped). This particular female had mated the previous year with a small Red-sided Garter snake (*T. sirtalis parietalis*) to produce a litter of twenty-one young intergrades of varying colours. Several were very clearly marked with red, others merely shades of brown like the mother, but most were somewhere between the extremes and showed slight tinges of red or orange in their markings. The melanistic youngsters were eventually mated amongst themselves and several all-black litters were born.

Due to the number of babies being produced, not only of Garter snakes, but also Water snakes, it meant that only a small proportion could be retained in the collection. The activities with the snakes was purely a leisure-time pursuit for the author, and it was found that somewhere in the region of one hundred and twenty to one hundred and forty snakes was the limit that he could maintain satisfactorily. Outlets for the surplus specimens were explored, and the snakes were soon accepted by zoological and private collections, often quite far afield. Reptile enthusiasts who had never bred any snakes were successful with youngsters born in the author's collection. Specimens were supplied from time to time to a doctor at Bristol University who was engaged in research into snake muscles. Zoology students from the University were frequent visitors to discuss and purchase snakes. On occasions dealers bought a dozen babies at a time, but most were sold to boys (and sometimes girls) keen on natural history, and anxious to learn about snakes. Several leaflets were prepared as handouts, to give advice to those keeping snakes for the first time. Sometimes there would be a two hour discussion with a young boy buying a snake (for the equivalent of $1.00), but it is considered that the time spent in giving advice and encouraging young people to study snakes was worthwhile in helping to promote a better understanding of these much maligned and misunderstood creatures.

12. SUMMARY OF BREEDING
EXPERIMENTS — WATER SNAKES

During April 1967 came the first success with American Water snakes, when a mating was obtained between a male Broad-banded Water snake (*Natrix sipedon confluens*) and a large female Northern Water snake (*Natrix sipedon sipedon*). Both of these had been purchased when adult. The result of this cross, in July, was a litter of twenty (sixteen alive) intergrade youngsters. The best six (four females and two males) were selected for rearing.

As the baby snakes were all strong and healthy, selection was made on the basis of the most attractive or distinctive coloring or markings. The actual appearance of these babies and their relation to the markings of the parents are detailed in the next chapter.

As with most of the American Water snakes the bright banded markings of the baby specimens became less distinct with age, but in spite of this they all retained clear traces of the bands into adult life. Several of the more reddish-marked specimens became more colorful with age. All thrived and were, at eight months old, sixteen to eighteen inches in length.

At thirteen months old the biggest (and best colored) pair of youngsters mated, and in January 1969 a small litter of eleven (one dead) second generation crosses were born.

This pair of first generation crosses produced four litters before the female died suddenly from causes unknown. The dates of mating, dates of births and sizes of litters are as follows:—

	MATING		BIRTH DATE		SIZE OF LITTER	BORN ALIVE
1.	8 September	1968	20 January	1969	11	10
2.	4 June	1969	6 October	1969	17	17
3.	14 April	1970	12 August	1970	28	27
4.	11 January	1971	15 June	1971	23	18

The male of this pair was a particularly virile specimen and fathered all litters of second generation crosses, mating regularly with all of the four females kept. As can be imagined, only a selected few babies could be kept, and the practice was to retain the reddest marked specimens from the litters produced by the female whose litters have been detailed, and sell the balance.

The original female Northern Water snake mated with the same Broad-banded male in October 1968 and produced a litter of intergrades (eighteen babies — seventeen alive) in February 1969. A previous mating toward the end of 1967 with a younger and much smaller Broad-banded male had only resulted in the deposition of a large mass of decomposed babies.

Going back to 1967, the other Water snake success was a litter of Broad-banded Water snakes born to a pair of snakes purchased as hatchlings two years previously. The female was only twenty-six inches long at the time of the birth, and the litter was small (eight young — six alive).

Between 1968 and 1971 litters of Water snakes were a regular event. Apart from the second generation intergrades more Broad-banded Water snakes were born, and also one of the female Northern/Broad-banded first generation crosses was mated back to a Broad-banded male, producing babies which in general appearance had lost any Northern Water snake characteristics.

13. HEREDITY AND THE INTERGRADATION OF SUB-SPECIES

The study of heredity and genetics is a complicated one and it is only proposed to touch briefly upon aspects which may concern the snake breeder. The appearance of an animal does not necessarily reveal its heredity. Each fertilized egg which develops into an animal has chromosomes from both parents, and these determine inheritance. Although sometimes their effects are obvious they can quite often be disguised. When a black (melanistic) and a normal striped Garter snake are mated, the offspring receive a chromosome bearing the factor (gene) for melanism from one parent, and one bearing the factor for normal striped skin pattern from the other. However, all the young will appear striped. This is because the black factor is recessive and is masked by the dominant gene for the striped pattern. These offspring which are genetically mixed for colour will, when mated, produce young in the ratio of three striped to one black. To take it one stage further, mating a black Garter snake to a striped specimen which possesses the recessive black factor will result in fifty per cent of the resultant babies being black. The diagram page 56 explains this. The discovery that the melanism in Garter snakes is a straightforward Mendelian recessive factor was made by the Blanchards(see Further Reading). Obviously, mating black snakes together can only result in all young being black.

It is quite probable that the factor for albinism is also a straightforward recessive factor, as this would be indicated by a report in the International Zoo Year Book (Volume 9. Published by Zoological Society of London, 1969.) on reptile breeding re-

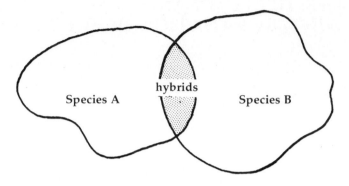

If the range of two species overlap, and the two interbreed, the offspring hybrids are nearly always sterile.

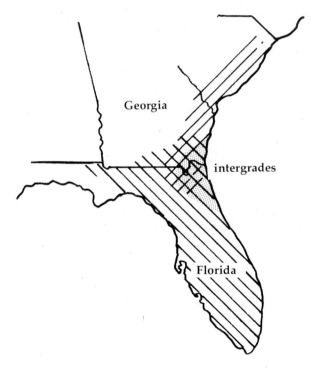

Red Rat Snakes from South Carolina are much prized for their deep russet color, Floridian Red Rat snakes have a much duller brownish cast. Where the ranges of these two color forms overlap, 'color intergrades' result. Were these populations ssp, the crosses would be true intergrades.

cords at Baltimore Zoo, Maryland. An interesting account is given of breeding albino Corn snakes (*Elaphe guttata guttata*) over a period of several years. The Zoo started with a pair of normal marked specimens which had been the result of a captive mating between a normal female and an albino male. The ratios of normal colored and albino young after the first generation, were similar to that which could be anticipated when dealing with the melanistic Garter snakes.

Working on these principles, once a snake breeder has just one albino or melano snake he knows that he can produce more of either type two generations on. Although the author did not have an opportunity to prove the theory, he considers it likely that a melano Garter snake (provided it was *Thamnophis sirtalis ssp.*) could be used to produce color true examples of any of the other *Thamnophis sirtalis* sub-species. As a melano snake's color genes would have to be for black only they could not influence the color genes (which would be dominant) of its mate. This could be useful to produce other sub-species of the genus when only one specimen of a type is available. For example, a herpetologist with just one specimen of the rare San Francisco Garter snake, could mate it to a melano Eastern Garter and produce babies all with the appearance of normal San Francisco Garter snakes, but, of course, carrying in their cells the recessive black factor. There could be no color factor in the black snake's makeup to affect or dominate the color genes of its mate.

Intergrades between an Eastern and a Red-sided Garter snake produced a variety of coloration in the young which was, to a large extent, a blending of the color characteristics of each parent. These snakes intergrade naturally in the wild where their ranges overlap. The babies showed varying degrees of coloring from the bright red of one parent to the brown and yellow of the other. Most were intermediate, being brownish with three yellow stripes and orange-red markings laterally.

The intergrading of the Northern Water and the Broad-banded Water snakes discussed in Chapter 12 also produced babies that were a compromise between the colors and skin patterns of the parents. The Northern Water snake has a small number of bands around the anterior part of its body (that is,

INHERITANCE OF MELANISM IN THAMNOPHIS.

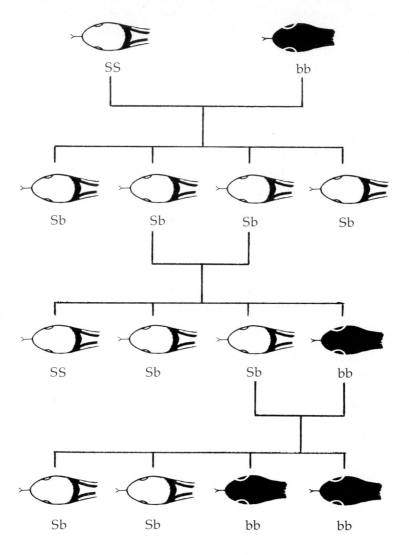

S= Dominant Striped Factor.   b= Recessive Black Factor.

bands reaching the ventral plates on each side), and this is followed by dorsal bands across the top of the body only, which alternate with lateral blotches. Counting the bands along the backbone gives a total of over thirty in all cases. The Broad-banded Water snake has but eleven to seventeen bands which are complete to the ventrals, with no separate lateral blotches. Ventrally the average Northern Water snake has a design of reddish half-moon markings in a fairly regular pattern, whereas the Broad-banded is heavily marked with brick-red patterns which form squarish shapes. The Broad-banded also possesses a distinct dark stripe from the eye to the angle of the jaw, which is not present in the Northern Water snake.

The intergrade babies resembled the Northern Water snake at first sight, but the markings counted along the backbone were less, totalling only twenty-one to twenty-six, and of these just the anterior five to nine were complete bands to the ventrals. The ventral markings were, on most specimens, fairly irregular in pattern, but neither of half-moons or of squarish format. The eyestripe was present to some degree in all but one or two snakes, and these were the ones with the reddest background color. These intergrades were a compromise between the two distinct pattern types of the parents, having the general appearance of Northern Water snakes, but with dorsal markings reduced in number; ventral pattern somewhere between the two, and most snakes showing at least some trace of an eyestripe.

As expected, the second generation families produced by these intergrades showed a very wide variety of marking and coloration. There was a tendency for the second generation young to have complete crossbands all the way down the body, although the number stayed between the twenty-one to twenty-six limit. More specimens showed evidence of eyestripes than did not. Ventrally, the variation was wide and took many forms too numerous to detail. The extremes were from almost unmarked pale color to a very dark unmarked mauve, with the majority displaying a bewildering variety of spots, blotches, squares and even longitudinal stripes. One of the interesting facets of these breeding experiments was that it was just not possible to predict the markings or color of an expected litter of snakes.

One thing that was noticed about the intergrade Water snakes was with regard to their disposition. Although they would snap and strike wildly when being fed, at other times they were invariably docile and easy to handle. On the other hand, the baby Broad-banded Water snakes were inclined to strike at fingers all the time, and were averse to being handled. When an intergrade was mated back to a true Broad-banded and the babies resembled Broad-banded Water snakes (although with more than the "correct" number of crossbands), they also appeared to inherit their aggressive behaviour.

14. RELEASES IN THE WILD

If the snake breeder has any success with his efforts, the question of possible release of specimens can arise, either because there is the desire to found a colony of snakes at a particular site, or merely because there are just too many baby snakes to tend.

At one time the author had plans to establish several colonies of either garter or water snakes in locations around his hometown in Bristol, England. It was felt that such introductions would provide a welcome supplement to the meagre list of indigenous snake species in the British Isles (three only).

The first selected site was a small area between a river and an old quarry, where grass snakes (*Natrix natrix helvetica*) had previously been seen and captured. Their presence indicated an amphibian food supply available probably adequate to support a small number of snakes. In August 1967 ten young garter snakes and eight newly hatched Italian grass snakes were released. Subsequent events proved this to be an ill-chosen site, as early the next year, following work on a nearby motor highway, the area was used as a dumping ground for the debris from demolished houses and the whole site disappeared under about six feet of bricks and rubble. Although a number of visits were made (fairly regularly, as the nearby river provided a useful supply of minnows) no snakes were ever seen there again.

After this unsuccessful attempt to enrich the United Kingdom reptile life, thoughts turned to a possible introduction of water snakes (the author's own intergrade specimens) in the

Mendip Hills a few miles southeast of Bristol. There was already a good population of reptiles and amphibians here. In spring the land surrounding certain ponds would be alive with frogs and toads, and in dryer parts on the grassy slopes the venomous adder (*Vipera berus*), viviparous lizard (*Lacerta vivipara*) and the legless lizard known as the slow-worm (*Anguis fragilis*) were very much in evidence. Grass snakes were also present although not often observed. The plan was briefly discussed with Professor Bellairs (Reader in Embryology in the University of London, Honorary Herpetologist to the Zoological Society of London and one-time editor of the "British Journal of Herpetology" and as a result the project was abandoned. It was considered that the effect, if the introduction flourished, on the local grass snake population was very much an unknown quantity and the existing balance of reptile and amphibian life in the district could be severely affected. The area is now a nature reserve with full protection for all fauna and flora, so in this case the right decision was made.

As a rule introductions of foreign animals of any sort to a country are usually regarded in retrospect with some regret. A few examples are the rabbit to Australia, and the American grey squirrel and mink to the United Kingdom. The grey squirrel causes serious damage to trees and is considered a pest for this reason alone, but it has also been the cause of near extinction for the native red squirrel. Introductions are not necessarily deliberate; the mink for instance, now a serious menace to wildlife along rivers and streams in certain areas and relentlessly hunted because of this, has established itself from escapees from mink fur farms.

Reptiles and amphibians do not seem to have figured to any great extent or with much degree of success in the field of introductions. In England since about 1900 various attempts have been made to introduce mainly European reptiles and amphibians, but usually any small colonies have existed for a short while and then gradually died out. To a large extent weather conditions could be blamed for this, as although adult specimens have been capable of withstanding the normal English climate the summers are not long enough or warm enough to permit breeding. It is, however, interesting to note that some success has been achieved with sub-species of European wall lizards. Two notable instances are worth mentioning. In 1932 a dozen common wall lizards (*Lacerta m. muralis*) were released in a Surrey locality containing old walls, and two further specimens the next year, and in 1951 a thriving breeding colony was observed. The second involved another sub-species (*Lacerta muralis nigriventris*) where fifteen specimens set free in South Devon around 1954 established themselves and bred annually. Ten years later the colony was reported to be several hundred strong.

With regard to snakes there appears to be no records of any serious attempt to introduce a foreign species. Any snakes found have been considered merely isolated escapes from captivity, apart from one case where a dealer apparently released a number of Dark green snakes (*Coluber jugularis*) when these were unsaleable.

An amphibian introduction to Australia approximately forty years ago which proved rather too successful was the giant Marine toad (*Bufo marinus*) of South America. Australian cane growers imported a consignment of these in the hope of controlling the grey-backed cane beetle which did great damage to the crops. Within three years *Bufo marinus* was a common feature of many cane towns, causing the death of many cats and dogs unwise enough to try eating them. The effect on wildlife outside cities was not good either. The attractive green tree frog (*Hyla caerulea*) disappeared from the vicinity of canefields, and numbers of Ibis and black snakes, one-time common swamp denizens, died after eating toads. No doubt there have been benefits insofar as the control of the cane beetle is concerned, but the price is a high one in terms of adverse effects on the native fauna.

When it is planned to release young captive-born snakes they will need to be marked and catalogued for positive identification when recaptured at a later date. A surprising number of snakes have slight abnormalities of the ventral scaling and if these are noted and a diagram recorded then extra marking is unnecessary. Marking is effected by cutting small "V" shapes of skin from the ventral scutes and noting the scute number counted forward from the vent. By making cuts either side and including subcaudal scutes many combinations of marks are possible. The cuts must be entirely through the skin deep enough to make a recognizable scar. A dab of antiseptic on such cuts is a wise move to prevent infection. Making these cuts on a baby snake is a delicate operation and great care must be exercised.

With snake species that have a patterned throat identification records could be made by means of photographs. In 1949 Carl Edalstam of Stockholm, Sweden, presented a paper to a British Herpetological Society meeting on his methods of research and study of snakes on a nature reserve outside his hometown. He was concerned with a population, within an area of about one square mile, of three hundred grass snakes, thirty smooth snakes (*Coronella austriaca*) and thirty adders (*Vipera berus*). Most of these he identified by photographing the color pattern in the region of the throat (for the smooth snake, the back). Such patterns he considered as an infallible guide to identity since, like fingerprints, no two were alike and they remained constant throughout life. For the adders, because of a high proportion of melanism, the removal of subcaudal scales was used for marking.

It is important in the United States that releases should only be of species or sub-species native to the area. To add specimens to a dwindling population or re-introduce a sub-species to an area within the recorded range where it had at one time been present is certainly admissible, but before any release is made of snakes from other areas or "unnatural" intergrades (that is, intergrades which could not possibly occur in the wild) much thought is necessary. Releases must not be made at the expense of existing reptile colonies, or where they are likely to cause trouble in the future for taxonomists involved in the preparation of range maps. If there is any doubt at all in the mind of the snake breeder whether or not the release of certain specimens is a wise move then advice should be sought from the local Wildlife Authorities.

APPENDIX 1

Reprinted from British Journal of Herpetology — June 1962.

NOTES ON THE GARTER SNAKE (*THAMNOPHIS SIRTALIS*), WITH PARTICULAR REFERENCE TO GROWTH AND BREEDING. By Robert J. Riches.

In August, 1957, a gravid female Garter snake was purchased from a dealer, and two weeks later (on the 18th August) it gave birth to eighteen young ones, three of which were born dead. The litter was produced early in the afternoon of a very hot sunny day. Several of them were deposited still in transparent membranes from which they emerged almost immediately. The average length of the fifteen living baby snakes was 162mm. (approx. 6⅜ inches) and all were extremely lively.

The babies commenced feeding two days later when they accepted earthworms very readily. As a supply of small fish or frogs was not available the baby snakes were fed solely on earthworms, and after a period of two months or so several of the young snakes were beginning to show signs of a rickety condition, and a number of them died as the condition became more serious. It was at this point that it became possible to obtain a constant supply of small minnows and the remaining snakes soon began to grow with this more satisfactory form of diet.

GROWTH

Two of the small snakes were, shortly after birth, given to a friend, and these specimens (which subsequently proved to be a true pair) were fed almost solely on minnows from the outset. The female of this pair increased in length and bulk very rapidly, and the following is a note of measurements taken over a period of two years.

28th September 1957 .... 260mm.
28th February   1958 .... 364mm.
27th March   1958 .... 405mm.
24th April   1958 .... 450mm.
19th July   1958 .... 600mm.
27th September 1958 .... 610mm.
20th March   1959 .... 630mm.
9th April   1959 .... 650mm.
2nd August   1959 .... 710mm.
3rd October   1959 .... 740mm.

The rate of growth of the male snake was not so great, but as adult male Garter snakes are normally considerably smaller than adult females this was only to be expected. The measurements of the male were as follows:—

15th September 1957 .... 193mm.
2nd March   1958 .... 250mm.
30th April   1958 .... 350mm.
15th June   1958 .... 440mm.
27th September 1958 .... 470mm.
20th March   1959 .... 470mm.
15th April   1959 .... 480mm.

This specimen died at the end of April, 1959, the cause being unknown. By comparing the tables of measurements it can be seen that the female snake had attained the length of two feet in only eleven months; the male at this time being approximately eighteen inches long and of a much slimmer build.

It must be stated that these snakes were not allowed to hibernate either in the winter of 1957/58 or 1958/59.

BREEDING

In their second winter (1958/59) both snakes were kept in a heated vivarium with the only two other survivors of the litter; a female approximately eighteen inches long and a very dark coloured male between fifteen and sixteen inches in length. On numerous occasions the small dark coloured male made attempts to mate with the large female, who was then over two feet long and quite a bulky snake. No successful mating was observed, or in any case expected, as both snakes were considered to be too

64

young. It should also be mentioned at this point that the dark male Garter snake also made attempts at times to mate with several young Grass snakes (*Natrix natrix*).

In April, 1959, the large female was separated from the other snakes and put into an outdoor vivarium of the garden frame type. Within a few months it became apparent that the snake was gravid and on August 16th sixteen young ones were produced.

The next winter, 1959/60, this snake (together with the dark coloured male and the other small female) was allowed to hibernate in the outdoor vivarium. In the spring the dark male was observed to be mating with the largest female very soon after emergence from hibernation. A litter of forty-five young ones was born on August 16th (the same date as the previous year). Two further young were produced, still-born, a week later.

SUMMARY

It appears that under favourable conditions in captivity a female Garter snake can attain a length of two feet in under one year. The rate of growth of the particular female specimen for which a table of measurements has been given is perhaps exceptional, and it must be admitted that it has not been possible subsequently, even with the same vivarium conditions and using the same diet, to rear a specimen to over eighteen inches in length in the first twelve months of its life.

Pope (1956) states that a female Garter snake is capable of producing its first litter in its second summer. In the case of the litter born on August 16th, 1959, it would appear that prevention of hibernation for the two previous winters had no effect at all on the fertility of the male and female snakes concerned.

AUTHOR'S NOTE:— This article was written following the very first attempts to breed these snakes. Subsequent work several years later proved that a large proportion of baby snakes could be successfully reared, and also it was not exceptional to get a specimen to over two feet long within twelve months from birth.

APPENDIX 2

Reprinted from British Journal of Herpetology — Vol. 4, No. 1. 1967.
EARLY MATURITY IN GARTER SNAKES *(THAMNOPHIS ELEGANS ELEGANS)*

by Robert J. Riches.

Thamnophis species in their natural state usually become sexually mature at two and a half years, the females giving birth to their first litters when approximately three years old. If enough growth is attained young may be produced in the second year (Carpenter 1952). These observations involved the three Michigan species *Thamnophis sirtalis sirtalis, Thamnophis butleri* and *Thamnophis sauritus sauritus*, but it reasonable to assume that similar criteria apply to other species and sub-species in the genus. Prevention of hibernation under captive conditions does not inhibit breeding activity or prevent a female from producing young at the age of two years (Riches 1962). Sexual maturity depends on size attained rather than age.

From a litter of *Thamnophis elegans elegans* born in the author's collection on the 25th of August, 1965, a male and female specimen attained sexual maturity in just over eight months after being kept active and feeding through their first winter. Mating, which involved actual coupling for a period of one hour and forty-five minutes, occurred on the 6th of May, 1966. According to Blanchard (1942) observations on *Thamnophis sirtalis sirtalis* revealed the duration of attachment varied from five to thirty minutes, although unusually short copulations did not produce young.

At the date of mating the male snake measured 525mm.

(body length 381mm.) and the female 587mm. (body length 447mm.), the latter's tail being incomplete with approximately 12mm. missing.

Eight young were deposited on the 18th August, one week before the parents were twelve months old. Four were stillborn although fully developed and another merely a minute decomposed embryo, yet far enough advanced to show traces of skin pigmentation. The smallest full-term snake measured 138mm. and the largest 164mm. The litter born in 1965, which included the parent snakes, had consisted of twelve young, whose sizes ranged from a minimum of 200mm. to a maximum of 230mm. There is considerable difference among broods of *Thamnophis sirtalis sirtalis* in the average length of newborn snakes (Blanchard 1942). This evidently also applies to *Thamnophis elegans elegans*. The three living snakes were quite weak and two died with in twenty-four hours. The survivor, believed to be a male, is still thriving at the time of writing (October 1966).

APPENDIX 3

NOTES ON SEXUAL BEHAVIOUR IN FEMALE SNAKES
by Robert J. Riches — Nov. 1972.

The mating behaviour of the typical Colubrid snake is usu-ally a fairly standardized performance, with the male rubbing his chin along the female's back and matching the contours of her body with his own. Spasmodic muscular rippling movements then pass like waves forward from his tail to head. A loop of his body is then pushed underneath the female to bring her tail into a suitable position to facilitate the insertion of one hemipenis. Actual coupling may occur after only brief preliminary courtship, or may be a prolonged procedure depending on many factors such as temperature, weather, time of year, etc. A female may sometimes need extended courtship play before she will allow coupling, and indeed it appears that if she is reluctant to mate she can quietly resist copulation indefinitely. This means the female can either passively accept, or equally passively reject, copula-tion; although if she is definitely averse to any attention from a male (possibly through her immaturity, or by reason of the fact that she has already mated) she may take flight to escape the male violently lashing her tail or vibrating her tail-tip.

References to aggressive sexual behaviour on the part of a female snake are hard to find, so presumably it is not often witnessed. Behaviour of this kind is described by the Blanchards (1942) in relation to the Garter snake *(Thamnophis sirtalis sirtalis)*, but it is stated that such behaviour is exceedingly rare. The author has recently completed approximately six years work on control-led breeding and sub-species crossbreeding of American Water *(Natrix)* and Garter *(Thamnophis)* snakes and has witnessed many matings. On only two occasions has any behaviour been ob-

68

served on the part of a female snake which could be construed as actively inviting a male to mate. Both instances involved Garter snakes, and in each case, the female upon becoming aware of the male in her cage, crawled over him making convulsive pushing movements, and lifting her tail to expose the vent. Coupling took place almost immediately with very little preliminary courting by the male.

It has been recorded that in certain species a male will grasp a female in his jaws during courtship. This behaviour has been recorded by a number of observers, particularly in relation to King snakes *(Lampropeltis)* and various varieties of the Gopher and Bull snakes *(Pituophis)*, and reported by the Wrights (1957). The following observations relate to King snakes in the author's collection, and a brief note of their known histories may be of interest. The female Chain King snake *(Lampropeltis getulus getulus)* was purchased in November 1965. At a length of just over sixteen inches she was presumably one of the previous summer's hatchlings. By mid-1972 this snake was around five feet in length and very heavily built. Up to this time it had never been in contact with a male *Lampropeltis*. A male California King snake *(Lampropeltis getulus californiae* — banded phase) approximately four feet long was purchased in July 1972. The previous owner had advised that this snake had been caged alone in view of its aggressive attitude toward other snakes of its own species. When, on the 2nd July, the male was introduced into the cage already containing the female her reaction was immediate, with violently twitching body she bit the male twice just behind the head, and held on for a few seconds each time. At the same time she was pressing close to the male following the contours of his body with her own and, in fact, behaving as if she were the male. The male snake made many attempts to escape by moving forward but was followed closely by the female who maintained her position alongside him. This continued for about thirty minutes with the male displaying no sexual interest in the female, but merely making agitated jerky movements and continually moving around the cage. Several times the female by pushing her body hard against the male managed to force the tail end of his body up and over her own. At this time her tail would be raised high with the vent open and exposed, as with side to side movements she smeared small amounts of a thick creamy liquid across the male's back. As it was obvious that the male was not interested in mating, he was then removed from the cage. Attempts were made to secure a mating on several subsequent occasions, but although the male sometimes showed an initial interest in the female this appeared to evaporate well before there was any chance of coupling. At all times the female showed more interest in the male than he did in her. On all occasions except one, the two snakes were observed the whole time they were together. On the odd single occasion they were left unobserved for thirty minutes, but both snakes were carefully examined after this and no evidence was found to suggest that copulation had taken place.

Some weeks later it was obvious from the size of the Chain King snake that she was full of eggs. She became very restless on the 19th August, and on the 21st deposited thirty infertile eggs, all of which were softshelled, greasy looking and full of a thick yellow fluid.

It is believed that no mating took place but that the introduction of the male, which caused such a violent reaction from the female, triggered off a series of events in the female's body which resulted in the enlargement and deposition of the unfertilized eggs.

According to reports (from a number of observers) quoted by the Wrights (1957), the maximum size of a clutch for *Lampropeltis getulus getulus* is twenty-four eggs, and even less for *Lampropeltis getulus californiae*. It is therefore a great pity these particular eggs were infertile, as it would appear to be the biggest *Lampropeltis* clutch recorded.

Note: References quoted are from
    Sources in Recommended Reading: page 75.

APPENDIX 4

NOTES ON THE BREEDING OF *ELAPHE OBSOLETA ROS-SALLENI* IN CAPTIVITY.

by Robert J. Riches — August 1972.

A female Everglades Rat snake approximately five feet in length was purchased (with five other smaller specimens and one three-foot Florida King snake) from Thompson's Zoo, Clewiston, Florida on 22 July 1971.

The snake laid sixteen eggs (while still in a linen bag) in Decatur, Illinois on 28 July. These were put in plastic margarine containers with damp paper tissues as incubation media. The containers were placed on top of a domestic basement boiler, near the pilot light where the temperature was a constant 85 degrees Fahrenheit. Unfortunately, the boiler "kicked-on" several days later burning the eggs hard.

All the snakes were brought back to England in August 1971 and kept in heated vivaria.

Mating was observed on 5 April 1972 between this female and the largest male — a four-foot specimen of yellowish coloration. Prior to this the male, although sharing the female's quarters, had shown no interest in her.

For two or three days before egg laying the female was very restless, moving continually around the cage and eventually rubbing a raw spot on her snout. On 22nd May she laid twenty-two eggs, taking from 7:30 a.m. until just before 6:00 p.m. to complete the task. The eggs were varied in size and shape. Some were elongate and pointed at one end whereas others were almost completely spherical. An average egg measured 40 x 25 mm. The eggs were incubated in small plastic containers,

71

with three to five eggs to each container. Damp paper tissues were used once again as incubation media.

Three eggs were observed to have deep grooves forming on 13th June, but after about thirty-six hours in damp sand they filled out again. Two further eggs started to collapse on 28th June, but water loss made up after a period buried in damp sand.

During whole period of incubation the eggs were kept at a temperature between 78 and 85 degrees F.

On 7th-8th July one egg collapsed and filled out again several times and as it was thought to be "dead" it was opened. It contained a well-formed male snake 226mm. (just under nine inches) in total length (180mm. snout to vent). Formation of scales and pattern of dark blotches dorsally easily visible, although specimen semi-transparent. This snake was alive and movements made for some time after removal from egg.

25th July — Eggs examined — four slits noticed in egg with green stains. No snake visible but froth exuding from slits. Egg removed into case with damp moss at 10:30 a.m. Head emerged for an inch, then quickly withdrawn. Egg examined again at 1:30 p.m. Snake free of egg and very mobile. Pale greyish with darker markings. When handled immediately attempted to strike with head flattened, "S" coil and vibrating tail. Very plump with obviously large amount of yolk still in body.

26th July — Three eggs noticed with slits at 1:00 p.m. Put into cage with moss to emerge in their own time.

27th July — 7:30 a.m. three snakes still in eggs. One emerged after being disturbed, and two others emerged later in morning. One is deformed having three or four spinal kinks. All babies very bloated with yolk. 11:00 p.m. — further egg with slit (this egg had developed a growth of green fungus, circular and approximately 10mm. in diameter seven days previously).

28th July — Snake emerged from formerly fungussed egg at 9:00 a.m. while being examined. Two more eggs slit. 3:00 p.m. — Two slit eggs disturbed and babies emerged. One short-bodied and deformed.

29th July — Two slit eggs seen late the previous night; babies emerged during morning. One severely collapsed egg opened —

contained fully developed, but very small snake 211mm. in total length. Another collapsed egg opened — contained lively, but deformed, baby. Two collapsed eggs opened 5:00 p.m. One youngster deformed and dead — the other normal and lively enough to strike at fingers. This snake later lost strength rapidly and died during night.

30th July — Four eggs with slits. One baby emerged and after seeming dead for a while commenced breathing. Slightly kinked spine. Three others emerged during afternoon — all perfect. Only four eggs left now.

1st August — One egg slit in morning — baby left egg on evening and struck at fingers while still emerging.

5th August — One baby emerged from egg slit previous evening. As the remaining two eggs were discolored and collapsing they were opened. Both contained deformed and dead young.

The young snakes shed between 6th and 13th August. After shedding the dorsal blotches were much lighter in color and the ground color (previously light grey) was showing signs of a pinkish orange suffusion, particularly around the edges of any darker markings. Most of the young snakes were quite irritable in disposition and would strike repeatedly if attempts were made to handle them.

SUMMARY

A clutch of 22 eggs was laid by a five-foot Everglades Rat snake, following a mating seven weeks previously. The eggs were incubated in damp paper tissues in small plastic containers and maintained at a temperature of 78 to 85 degrees Fahrenheit. One egg was opened following collapse after 47 days incubation and was found to contain a well developed living embryo.

Hatching of the eggs took place after 64 to 75 days incubation. Some baby snakes were deformed, having spinal kinks which made normal locomotion difficult. Thirteen babies were normal (although one of these died soon after hatching), four had spinal deformities and four eggs did not hatch. These contained fully developed dead young, one of which had spine and head deformities, two with spinal kinks only and one apparently normal but very small.

APPENDIX 5

"ABIDEC" AQUEOUS MULTIVITAMIN SOLUTION

Produced by Parke, Davis & Company, Pontypool, Monmouthshire, U.K.

Each 0.6 ml. of this solution represents:—

Vitamin A	4000 I.U.
Vitamin D	400 I.U.
Vitamin B^1	1 mg.
Vitamin B^2	0.4 mg.
Vitamin B^6	0.5 mg.
Nicotinamide	5 mg.
Ascorbic Acid	50 mg.

RECOMMENDED READING & REFERENCES

Allen, R. (1971) How to Keep Snakes in Captivity. Great Outdoors Publishing Co. Florida.

Blanchard, F.N. & F.C. (1941) Factors Determining Time of Birth in the Garter Snake, Thamnophis sirtalis sirtalis (Linn.). Mich. Acad. Sci. Arts & Letters.

Blanchard, FN. & F.C. (1941) The Inheritance of Melanism in the Garter Snake, Thamnophis sirtalis sirtalis (Linn.). Mich. Acad. Sci. Arts & Letters.

Blanchard, F.N. & F.C. (1942) Mating of the Garter Snake, Thamnophis sirtalis sirtalis (Linn.). Mich. Acad. Sci. Arts & Letters.

Carpenter, C.C. (1952) Growth and Maturity of the Three Species of Thamnophis in Michigan. Copeia No. 4, 237-43.

Carr, A. (1963) The Reptiles, Time, Inc.

Pope, C. H. (1956) The Reptile World. Routledge & Kegan Paul, London.

Wright, A.H. & A.A. (1957) Handbook of Snakes of the U.S. & Canada. Cornell University Press, New York.

HERPETOLOGICAL SOCIETIES

AMERICAN HERPETOLOGICAL SOCIETIES

American Society of Ichthyologists & Herpetologists.
Division of Reptiles
U.S. National Museum
Washington, D.C. 20560

Chicago Herpetological Society
2001 N. Clark Street,
Chicago, Ill. 60614
Publication bulletin quarterly

Kansas Herpetological Society
Topeka Zoological Park
635 Gage Blvd.
Topeka, Kansas 66606

New York Herpetological Society
P.O. Box 3945
Grand Central Station,
New York, N.Y. 10017

Additional information on American societies can be obtained from the publishers of Herpetological Review, 800 Wells St., Milwaukee, WI. 53233.

BRITISH HERPETOLOGICAL SOCIETY

Secretary:—Mrs. Monica Green, c/o Zoological Society of London, Regents' Park, London N.W.1, England.

President:—Dr. J. F. D. Frazer.

Society founded 1947. Publication "British Journal of Herpetology" issued at six-monthly intervals. Meetings held monthly.

INTERNATIONAL HERPETOLOGICAL SOCIETY

Secretary:— Malcolm Delingpole, "Fairfield" Radford Road, Alvechurch, Birmingham B48 7ST, England.

President:— James O. P. Ashe.

Society founded 1970. Publication "The Herptile" issued at approximately four-monthly intervals. Meetings held monthly.

Plate 1. Northern Water Snake. *(Natrix sipedon sipedon)* This is the adult female used in the intergradation experiments.

Plate 2. Broad-banded Water Snake. *(Natrix sipedon confluens)*. Eight month old female.

Plate 3. Northern/Broad-banded Water Snake intergrade. Three month old male.

Plate 4. Eastern Garter Snake. *(Thamnophis sirtalis sirtalis).* Melanic female.

Plate 5. Mountain Garter Snake. *(Thamnophis elegans elegans)*. Adult female.

Plate 6. Mountain Garter Snake, *(Thamnophis elegans elegans)*. Young male.

Plate 7. Eastern Garter Snake. *(Thamnophis sirtalis sirtalis)*. Adult female with typical striped pattern.

Plate 8. Eastern/Red-sided Garter Snake intergrade *(Thamnophis sirtalis sirtalis X sirtalis parietalis)*. Young female.

Plate 9. British Grass Snake *(Natrix natrix helvetica)*, hatching.

Plate 10. Newly hatched Viperine snake *(Natrix maura)*. This species is a harmless relative of the European grass snakes despite its popular name, which is obtained because of its superficial resemblance to the European Adder or Viper.

81

Plate 11. Newly-born Garter Snakes. *(Thamnophis s.sirtalis).* These two babies are from the same litter, one being the normal striped pattern, the other all-black or melanistic.

Plate 12. Close-up of head of intergrade Water Snake.

Plate 13. Second generation intergrade Water Snake.
Gravid female.

Plate 14. Newly hatched Everglades Rat Snake *(Elaphe obsoleta rossalleni)*. Note the juvenile blotched markings and general color - quite different from the orange/yellow background and four faint stripes of the adult.

Plate 15. Adult Everglades Rat Snake *(Elaphe obsoleta rossalleni)*.

Plate 16. The Author with pair of Florida King snakes (*Lampropeltis getulus floridana*), raised from hatchlings to sexual maturity in 14 months.

Plate 17. Newly hatched Florida King snake — one from above snakes' first litter.

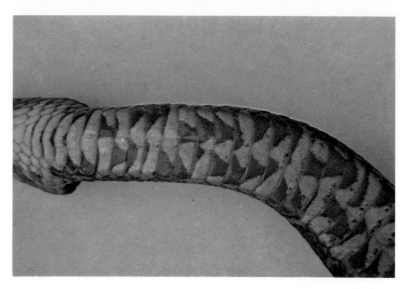

Plate 18. Northern/Broad-banded Water snake intergrade. Throat pattern of adult female.

Plate 19. Hatchling Italian Grass snake (*Natrix natrix natrix*). Two-striped variety.

Plate 20. Hatchling English Grass snake (*Natrix natrix helvetica*).

Plate 21. Northern/Broad-banded Water snake intergrades. Eleven-month old females.

Plate 22. Juvenile Everglades Rat snake (*Elaphe obsoleta rossalleni*).

Plate 23. Juvenile Corn or Red Rat snake (*Elaphe guttata guttata*).

INDEX

89